Getting Into Mini-Reefs

JIM FATHERREE

Contents

Photos by the author unless specifically noted otherwise

© T.F.H. Publications, Inc.

Distributed in the UNITED STATES to the Pet Trade by T.F.H. Publications, Inc., 1 TFH Plaza, Neptune City, NJ 07753; on the Internet at www.tfh.com; in CANADA by Rolf C. Hagen Inc., 3225 Sartelon St., Montreal, Quebec H4R 1E8; Pet Trade by H & L Pet Supplies Inc., 27 Kingston Crescent, Kitchener, Ontario N2B 2T6; in ENGLAND by T.F.H. Publications, PO Box 74, Havant PO9 5TT; in AUSTRALIA AND THE SOUTH PACIFIC by T.F.H. (Australia), Pty. Ltd., Box 149, Brookvale 2100 N.S.W., Australia; in NEW ZEALAND by Brooklands Aquarium Ltd., 5 McGiven Drive, New Plymouth, RD1 New Zealand; in SOUTH AFRICA by Rolf C. Hagen S.A. (PTY.) LTD., P.O. Box 201199, Durban North 4016, South Africa; in JAPAN by T.F.H. Publications. Published by T.F.H. Publications, Inc.
MANUFACTURED IN THE
UNITED STATES OF AMERICA
BY T.F.H. PUBLICATIONS, INC.

Introduction

In the last 20 years marine aquarium hobbyists have come to realize that it is possible to keep far more than just fish alive in our homes and offices. Prior to the last couple of decades it was generally regarded as very, very difficult to keep most reef-dwelling plants and animals alive in captivity, but that has now become commonplace. Industries and hobbyists alike around the world have developed the equipment and methods that make the keeping of reef dwellers possible not only for experts but also for beginners as well. Various aspects of keeping reef aquariums, from livestock collection techniques to our understanding of filtration, have improved, and anyone willing to learn and work can now become a successful reef keeper.

The range of plants and animals living in the reef environment is very wide, and there are now so many different types of organisms available at retail stores that hobbyists may feel overwhelmed. There is much to learn about each group of invertebrates and about each individual species within the groups.. Many reef organisms require intense light, while others require none. Some can touch their tankmates, while many others will kill anything they come into contact with. Some require regular feeding, others need nothing. Some are hardy and will live for decades, while many probably won't make it for a month. The point is that there is much to learn about what to choose for your aquarium and what each animal requires to keep it not just alive, but healthy. Your goal as a beginner is to find out as much as possible about each of them and their care in order to increase your odds of success.

Although at one time the keeping of anything other than fish and a few hardy crustaceans in a marine aquarium was thought to be a very chancy operation, today's greater understanding of the life processes that go on in the marine environment, coupled with improved aquarium equipment, allows present-day aquarists to maintain a wide range of reef-dwelling invertebrates; shown here are disc anemones of the genus Discosoma. *Photo by U. E. Friese*

This view of part of a 200-gallon mini-reef aquarium shows its condition 24 months after it was set up. The reef structure itself, composed of carefully arranged live rock, has become coated with various algae and invertebrates that of course were much less in evidence when the tank was first set up. Photo by George D. Beaumont.

It is critical that you develop a good understanding of not just your livestock but also the reef environment itself so that you can reproduce its water and lighting conditions inside an aquarium. A good understanding of filtration, water quality, and lighting is the foundation of success. Once you have learned what you can about those topics you then will be ready to build your own reef and stock your aquarium. Then you can enjoy the process of maintaining your creation and watching it change and grow for years to come. In the following sections of this book these basics of reefkeeping will be covered.

Re-creating Nature in Your Reef Aquarium

irst things first. As a hobbyist you must develop a keen understanding of what the natural reef environment is like and how to best reproduce such an environment within the confines of your aquarium. That is obviously the most crucial part of starting up your reef aquarium and keeping its inhabitants alive and healthy for an extended period of time. If you can master this reproduction of nature you can enjoy a wide variety of reef creatures for many, many years. Learning the basics of filtration, water quality, and lighting *before* you get started will be the key to your success.

FILTRATION

Reef environments worldwide are found in waters that tend to be exceptionally clear and free of excess suspended matter. Contrary to what you might think, these waters are also extremely low in nutrients. This means that there are very few chemicals or compounds present in the water that the plants and animals on the reef can use as nutrients. There are also few or no toxic or detrimental compounds in these waters. In order for you to maintain these conditions in your aquarium you must employ three types of filtration: mechanical, chemical, and biological.

The water in aquariums is usually made cloudy by a variety of suspended particles, most of which are created in the aquarium itself. Very little comes from the outside environment in the form of dust or other particles. The major contributor to clouded water is actually fecal matter produced by your fish, either whole or broken up into tiny pieces. Leftover fish food, dead microorganisms, and silt particles produced by the breakdown of rocks in the aquarium by boring and burrowing organisms also contribute. All of these types of particles are collectively called "detritus." In order to remove detritus from the aquarium and keep the water clear you should use some form of mechanical filtration. This is accomplished by using any type of filter specifically designed to trap and remove particles. To remove suspended particles mechanical filters typically use some sort of sponge, floss, or fiber filter medium that must be either cleaned or replaced on a regular basis. The regular removal of detritus by replacing or cleaning filter media is also very important for another reason. Detritus is very high in nutrients and therefore must be removed in

The power filter seen here in side view fitting snugly on the back of a mini-reef tank helps to keep the water clear.

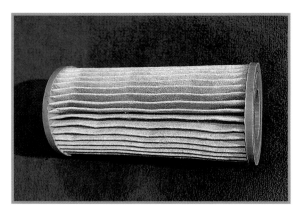

A used pleated cartridge filter designed for use with a canister filter. Cleaned properly, it can be used over and over.

order to keep overall nutrient levels low in the aquarium.

One of the most common types of mechanical filter is the outside hanging box filter. These filters hang on the aquarium, generally on the back, and typically contain filter floss, pads, or sponges. A quality box filter will run very quietly while doing an excellent job of removing much of the particulate matter in the water and will last for several years. As an added benefit, most do not require you to do any maintenance other than changing or cleaning the filter media. Models that use a sponge allow the sponges to be rinsed out and reused over and over instead of having to be replaced.

Another popular type of mechanical filter is the canister filter. These filters are typically constructed from a large plastic cylinder with an internal pump and filter sponge or cartridge. The canister usually sits underneath the aquarium; water is drawn down by an intake hose, forced through the filter media inside, and is then pumped back up to the aquarium through a return hose. Because canister filters usually are kept under the aquarium they are out of sight, but unfortunately this means that they can be quite troublesome when it comes time to replace or clean the filter media. It can be hard to get to it. The "hang on the tank" type of canister filter is similar to a box filter because it hangs off the back of the aquarium. These filters are easier to remove and service, and they work very well.

Many people forgo the expense of adding a mechanical filter to their reef aquarium. Surprisingly enough, most particulate matter will settle out of the water and collect in areas where there is very little or no water movement, leaving the aquarium's water relatively clear. The downside to this is that the settled material still has to be removed from the aquarium one way or another, which means that it will have to be done manually by using a siphon hose to suck out the excess detritus. This process will be discussed further in the maintenance section.

The reason that the detritus has to be removed—and removed as often as possible—from the aquarium is that it is important to keep nutrient levels as low as possible. This need to remove detritus as fast as possible is another reason that filters using sponges or reusable cartridges are better for the reef aquarist than those that don't. In aquariums that house only fish, nutrient levels are not as much of a concern, and mechanical filters that use replacement-type media are fine. However, you will not want to leave a replacement-type filter medium in use until it is

A prefabricated flow-through pouch of activated carbon; such pouches can be placed in filters so that water constantly flows over them.

GETTING INTO MINI-REEFS

really dirty, because it may take weeks before it "looks" to be in need of replacement. This is because much of the matter that it traps simply dissolves right back into the aquarium. But you won't want to buy new filters every few days to replace ones that look relatively clean, either. So stick to a sponge that can be rinsed as often as is necessary, or to a reusable cartridge that can be cleaned every few days and placed back into service.

You must also use chemical filtration as a means to further remove any nutrients or other pollutants from the aquarium's water. All of the animals in your aquarium will constantly produce unwanted nutrients in the form of wastes, but all nutrients are initially added from external sources such as fish food and impure water. Various chemicals may also enter the aquarium from

The foam and the liquid formed from it that have accumulated in the collection cup of a protein skimmer.

external sources, and although they may not be nutrients they are nevertheless unwanted.

To remove these things you need to use chemical filtration, the most basic method of which is using activated carbon. Activated carbon sucks up countless chemicals from the water, from heavy metals to naturally produced acids. You should buy high-quality carbon and use it by putting some in a mesh bag. The bag can then be placed in a location where water will do more than just run over it; you want the water to flow through it. You can also

A small venturi skimmer designed to hang off the back of an aquarium. The main body of the skimmer is outside the aquarium, but the pump that drives the skimmer is inside the tank.

use the foot cut off a pair of pantyhose by filling it up and tying a knot in the end. To get the best results, simply place the bag or hose inside your mechanical filter where there is a constant flow. How much carbon to use and how often it should be changed will be discussed in the following section on maintenance.

Another method of chemical filtration is the use of a protein skimmer, which is also called a foam fractionator by some. These devices may seem to be mechanical filters at first glance, but removing particulate matter is not their function. Instead they remove a variety of compounds from the water by means of adhesion. A skimmer is basically a cylinder that water is forced through. A column of tiny bubbles is produced inside the cylinder, and proteins, fatty acids, and other organic materials stick to the bubbles. The result is a thick foam of water bubbles and unwanted compounds. If you've been to the beach and seen a thick foam collecting on the shore, you've seen natural skimming; it's the same basic process. However, in a skimmer the foam is collected in a cup, where it turns into a thick, nasty liquid. This stuff can then be poured down the drain.

This venturi-style skimmer has been installed in a sump tank under the main aquarium. The skimmer is driven by a large pump that has been plumbed into the sump, thus providing a cleaner look by avoiding having hoses and other equipment hanging off the back of the tank; it also allows for the use of a larger skimmer.

There are two basic types of skimmers for you to consider, the counter-current skimmer and the venturi skimmer. In a counter-current skimmer water usually enters the cylinder from the top, with the bubbles being produced at the bottom through use of a small air pump and airstone. The water is forced downward, but the bubbles rise up through it to produce foam. Now the name "counter-current" makes sense! These skimmers do an exceptional job, but there are a couple of things to consider. First, the taller the skimmer the more contact time there is between the water and the bubbles. Short counter-current skimmers don't work nearly as well as tall ones, which means you'll want a tall one, which means that it will take up more space. The counter-current skimmer also requires the purchase of an air pump and airstone (which has to be replaced regularly). Venturi skimmers need no air pump and can be quite small. These skimmers make foam by forcing water through a specially designed valve (the venturi valve) that draws in air. This intake of air produces copious bubbles that are then swirled around at high speed inside the skimmer. As with the counter-current skimmers, the resultant foam is then collected in a cup. These skimmers are becoming more and more popular because they have less hardware and can be smaller in size.

While small skimmers, whether they be counter-current or venturi in design, can be hung off the back of small and medium-sized aquariums, larger skimmers on larger aquariums may require the use of a sump tank under the main aquarium. For such large aquariums it is common to have holes drilled through the bottom of the tank to allow plumbing lines to be run under the aquarium instead of behind it. In this case the lines run to a separate tank under the cabinet (the sump tank) where a skimmer can be hooked up and "hidden" from sight. This also allows for the use of very large pumps that can be plumbed to the sump and main aquarium to create strong circulation up in the aquarium and run the skimmer down the sump simultaneously.

Lastly, there are phosphate removers, which also are a great aid in chemical filtration. Phosphates are one of the dominant undesirable compounds created in the aquarium and commonly added from outside sources. Phosphates create health problems for some reef organisms, and they also encourage the growth of unwanted algae. High phosphate levels will quickly bring on the uncontrollable growth of green and brown algae all over the rocks and tank surfaces in your aquarium. Much phosphate is removed during mechanical filtration in the form of fish feces and food, and some is also removed by protein skimming, but in some cases this is not enough, and the use of a phosphate-removing product will be required. Like activated carbon, the best phosphate removers come in granular form. The granules can be poured into a mesh bag or into pantyhose and used just like carbon. In fact, it can be added to the same bag and mixed with carbon if you like.

Inside your aquarium the livestock also pollutes the water by producing toxic ammonia as a waste product of metabolism. Ammonia is also produced by the decay of fish foods, organic matter, and any dead tissues (such as a dead fish left in the aquarium). Ammonia *must* be removed from the aquarium before it becomes concentrated enough to cause the sickness or death of any of your livestock. The removal of ammonia is done through the use of biological filtration. Fortunately, various bacteria actually use ammonia and related substances as their food sources, hence the name "biological" filtration. What you must do is provide a home for these bacteria so that this biological removal of ammonia can be accomplished.

On the reef ammonia levels are effectively zero, because they are diluted by sea water and because bacteria convert the ammonia to other substances as quickly as it is produced. Therefore the concentration of ammonia in your aquarium should also stay at zero. On most marine aquariums special biological filters such as undergravel filters, rotating water contactors, and wet/drys must be employed to do the job. However, in reef aquariums none of these filters is needed, because bacteria will grow on and in the rough natural surface of the rocks you use to create your reef. The exact amount of rock needed is highly variable, depending on how much and what kind of livestock is added to the aquarium, but somewhere from 1 to 2 pounds of porous rock per gallon of aquarium water should be sufficient. Over a period of a few weeks the rocks will become completely colonized by bacteria and will continue to do their job indefinitely.

WATER QUALITY

Sea water is not simply salt and water mixed together. It is actually a soup of several elements and compounds, sodium chloride being only one of them. There are several high-quality brands of synthetic sea salt on the market now, all having the same desirable components of sea water in the proper proportions. Among these components there are a few elements that are constantly used up by the livestock in your aquarium. These are calcium, strontium, iodine, and a variety of trace elements, all of which must be added to the aquarium in a number of ways in order to keep their concentrations as close as possible to what they are in nature.

Live rock makes a great natural biological filter. Beneficial bacteria will colonize the highly porous irregular surface of the rock.

But first you must add the proper amount of synthetic sea salt to make up your aquarium's water. The saltiness, or salinity, of sea water around reefs varies relatively little from place to place and is relatively stable over time. So you will not only need to adjust the salinity of your aquarium water to the proper level but also will also need to keep it there. The saltiness of water is usually measured through use of a hydrometer to find its specific gravity. The hydrometer is a mandatory piece of equipment that you must purchase and learn to use. It may sound complicated, but it isn't. The specific gravity of aquarium water is simply a comparison of the mass of a given volume of aquarium water to the mass of the same volume of pure water at the same temperature. Pure water at room temperature has a specific gravity of 1.000 and is used as the reference; an equal volume of water with any dissolved salts or other chemicals in it will be at least slightly heavier and thus will have a higher specific gravity than pure water. Natural sea water has a specific gravity that varies from about 1.022 to 1.030. However, as water is made saltier and the specific gravity gets higher, the dissolved oxygen content of the water gets lower (it may be easier to think of the water as being "full of salt" and not leaving much room for oxygen and other gases to dissolve into it). For this reason it is best to keep the specific gravity in your aquarium closer to the lower limit of 1.022 than to the upper limit of 1.030 in order to keep oxygen levels as high as possible.

Many animals, such as corals, and a few plants must take in calcium from sea water for use in making their hard carbonate skeletons. On the reef ambient calcium concentrations are relatively high, at about 375 to 475 milligrams per liter (mg/l), compared to the concentration of other elements. It is best to maintain calcium levels in the aquarium optimally nearer the upper limit of 475 mg/l.

There are three ways to keep calcium levels that high. The first is by using liquid calcium additives. The most common types of liquid calcium additive are simply measured out according to the manufacturer's directions and added directly to the aquarium, typically on a weekly basis. They are thus very easy to use and are also hard to overdose. However, they are usually made by binding the calcium to an organic base that is left over after the calcium

Acropora formosa, *one of the reef-building staghorn corals that can benefit from calcium supplementation of their aquarium water.* Photo by Walt Deas

has been released and utilized. Over time this can lead to an accumulation of unwanted organic material in the aquarium unless it is controlled by use of an efficient protein skimmer. There also are newer liquid additives that come in two parts. These additives require you to add a first part to the aquarium, wait a short amount of time, then add the second component. They are a little more troublesome, but they work well.

A second method is the use of limewater, commonly called "kalkwasser," after the German name for it. Kalkwasser is made by adding powdered calcium hydroxide to fresh water, then adding the mixture to the aquarium. This should be done according to the manufacturer's directions, which are the same no matter what the brand. Basically, a small amount of the powder is added to a bucketful of fresh water and stirred vigorously. The solution is then allowed to rest for several hours so that any of the undissolved white powder can settle to the bottom. Then the top portion of the solution is poured into the aquarium,

The hard and soft corals are not the only reef dwellers that require calcium; hermit crabs like this Eupagurus bernhardus *also use it in manufacturing their chitinous exoskeletons.* Photo by MP and C. Piednoir, Aqua Press

leaving behind the milky portion that has formed in the bottom. Care must be taken to add the solution very slowly to the aquarium in an area of high water flow or the solution can cause unwanted side effects. This method sounds like a lot of trouble compared to using prefabricated additives, but it has some benefits that other additives don't. The chemistry of the limewater solution when combined with aquarium water helps maintain a high pH and high alkalinity levels (discussed below) when used correctly. These are very desirable side effects that are not seen with the use of liquid additives, and many feel that they make the extra work well worth it.

The third method is the use of a device called a calcium reactor. These devices add calcium to the aquarium water by dissolving calcium carbonate. This is done by injecting carbon dioxide (from a pressurized bottle) into a reactor filled with a crushed calcium carbonate sand. This causes the sand to very slowly dissolve into the aquarium water. Calcium reactors are complicated-looking contraptions and are usually somewhat expensive, but they are actually quite simple to use and are very effective.

Many reef inhabitants also use strontium in making their skeletons and apparently cannot thrive without it. Strontium is found at concentrations of 8 to 10 mg/l in sea water and thus should be maintained at about the same levels in the aquarium. There are several good prefabricated strontium additives available that should be used according to the manufacturer's directions. If a calcium reactor is used there is no need for adding strontium. Strontium levels will be maintained because strontium is released with calcium as the sand (which also has strontium in it) is dissolved within the reactor. Unfortunately, unlike calcium levels and many other water parameters, strontium levels cannot be easily verified by using test kits. It seems that no one has yet developed a simple (or maybe just affordable) method of accurately measuring strontium levels in aquarium water. So if you use additives, be sure

to follow directions and watch for signs of decreased skeletal growth that may be the result of a strontium deficiency.

While normally we all think of oxygen as being a good thing, it is produced in different forms during photosynthetic and metabolic processes within many reef organisms. Some forms can be very destructive and must be neutralized within the tissues in order to avoid problematic levels. To combat this potential toxic buildup, animals use iodine in complex processes to neutralize these forms of oxygen, making iodine another required element. Iodine is found in several forms in sea water at a concentration of about 60 parts per billion and can be added to the aquarium by using any of a wide variety of prefabricated liquid additives. Again, it is best to simply follow the manufacturer's directions with any of these products.

A natural reef scene in the Red Sea, one of the warmest oceanic areas. Water temperatures in tropical areas, although subject to fluctuations from season to season, generally change only minutely on a day-to-day basis. Photo by MP. and C. Piednor, Aqua Press

There are several other elements that are found in very low concentrations in sea water but are nevertheless important. However, because this group of "trace elements" includes several different individual elements found in very low concentrations, it is not practical to test their concentrations in aquarium water. Luckily, most are found in quality salt mixes and can be maintained in sufficient concentrations even if only small water changes are performed regularly. There are also several trace element additives available in liquid form and in blocks that slowly dissolve over a period of days or weeks when placed into the aquarium.

The water temperature around most coral reefs fluctuates between 70° and 85° F throughout the course of a year and is even more stable in many areas. So the water temperature of your reef aquarium should also stay within this range. However, because the dissolved oxygen level in an aquarium drops significantly as the water temperature increases, it is best to keep the temperature well under 85° F. Temperatures a little above 80° F are tolerable, but a temperature closer to 75° F is optimal. You should also keep in mind that while water temperatures fluctuate several degrees around reefs, the change is usually very slow. The temperature may vary much less than one degree per month as seasons change. Therefore the water temperature of your aquarium should be kept as stable as possible within the given range.

The pH of water is a number scale from 0–14 used to describe whether the water is acidic, basic, or neutral. Pure fresh water, which is neutral, has a pH of 7. Water with a lower pH is acidic, and water with a higher pH is basic. The pH in reef aquariums should always be somewhat basic, and it has been observed that many reef organisms can tolerate a pH of from about 7.6 to 9.0. However, the pH of sea water around most coral reefs varies only from 8.0 to 8.4. For this reason it is best to maintain a pH in your aquarium that stays within this same range.

The pH of aquarium water is primarily controlled by the concentration of dissolved carbon dioxide. If CO_2 concentrations are high the pH goes down; when CO_2 concentrations are low the pH goes up. Since the pH of natural sea water is basic, it is best to keep CO_2 concentrations relatively low in the aquarium. This is usually accomplished in marine aquariums simply by maintaining good water circulation and by keeping the water's surface agitated to promote gas exchange between the atmosphere and the aquarium. While it is very unusual, at times this is not enough to keep the pH within acceptable limits, and a pH buffer must be used. These buffers come in a variety of forms as both a liquid and a powder; just remember to add them slowly if they are required so that your livestock is not subjected to a harmfully rapid pH change that causes "pH shock."

Different lighting qualities in the same aquarium: above, only VHO actinic tubes (7100 degrees K) are being used; below, the same aquarium being lighted with the same actinic tubes, but with a pair of 5,500 K metal halide bulbs added to balance the color.

The alkalinity of water is a measure of how well it resists any rapid change in pH. As stated, the pH in an aquarium is strongly affected by the concentration of CO_2 in the water. Photosynthetic organisms use much of this CO_2 during the day, but at night photosynthesis stops and CO_2 levels go up. If the alkalinity is low this will lead to considerable fluctuations in the pH from day to night, which can be detrimental to the health of many reef organisms. Various other conditions can lead to similar problems over time, so it is important to keep the alkalinity within acceptable limits. There are two basic scales used for the same method of testing, the values being given in milliequivalents per liter (meq/l) or in carbonate hardness (dKH). For sea water around most coral reefs the alkalinity ranges from 2.1 to 2.5 meq/l, or 6 to 7 dKH. However, because aquariums tend by nature to be much more unstable than the oceans, an optimal alkalinity should be maintained a little higher than that of sea water. You should try to maintain an alkalinity between 2.5 and 3.5 meq/l, or 7 to 10 dKH. Unfortunately, over time alkalinity will almost always drop below those levels if it is not maintained through the addition of alkalinity buffers in powdered or liquid

form, so it must be monitored and adjusted as often as is necessary.

LIGHTING

Many of the animals that we put in reef aquariums have special relationships with microscopic algae. These algae actually live inside the tissues of the host, such as a coral or sea anemone, and help to provide the host with nutrients. This relationship makes the hosts dependent on the algae and thus makes them dependent on sunlight, which the algae use for photosynthesis. This relationship is discussed in more detail later, but for now it is important to realize that the type of lighting provided is the most important difference between "fish only" marine aquariums and reef aquariums. It is also important to remember that it is not enough for reef aquarium lighting systems to emit intense light for the purpose of mimicking sunlight. The light, in addition, must be light of a particular color in order to keep these organisms healthy.

Water acts as something of a filter that cuts out much of the red and yellow parts of the normal spectrum within the first few feet of depth in the ocean. That is why waters around corals reefs always have a blue color unless the depth is very shallow. The algae that live inside a host's tissue have adapted to this situation by being able to specifically use blue light for their photosynthetic processes. So if the basic idea is to use artificial lighting to reproduce the light that these algae are used to receiving, you should use lamps that emit less red and yellow light and more blue light to promote photosynthesis. However, at least some white light is also desirable so that the aquarium has a more natural look.

The color of the spectrum of any light source can be described in units called degrees Kelvin (°K). The more toward the yellow and red end of the spectrum the lower the Kelvin number, and the more toward the blue end of the spectrum the higher the Kelvin number. For example, yellowish street lights are usually 4,700°K, daylight is usually around 6,500°K, and blue aquarium tubes (which are known as "actinic" tubes because blue light is called actinic) are around 7,100°K. The optimal color lighting for a reef aquarium should be about the same as that of normal daylight or a little bluer, so you should use a lighting system that produces a bright light that is about 6,500°K to 6,800°K.

To do this you can use either of two basic methods. You can use tubes that are about 6,500°K, or you can use a combination of tubes that put out an overall color of about 6,500°K. The simplest of the two is obviously to buy lamps that put out 6,500°K; they are available in a variety of types. The fluorescent tubes known as "daylight tubes" will do, but

The stony corals in general, such as the open brain coral Trachyphyllia geoffroyi *shown here, are among the most demanding of marine invertebrates as far as the intensity and quality of the aquarium's lighting are concerned.* Photo by U. E. Friese

the metal halides that also put out this color are far brighter. Those that add blue to make them 6,800°K are usually called "actinic-day," "actinic-white," or "50/50" (which means they are half white and half blue). Any of these are great choices, but the other approach is still very common. In this case a combination of lamps is used, such as metal halides that are 5,500°K with fluorescents that are 7,100°K. Fluorescents of 5,500°K can

This prefabricated canopy uses a built-in fan to cool the two powerful compact fluorescent tubes it houses.

also be used with metal halide lamps that are 10,000°K, giving the aquarium a nice look as well. In most cases, prefabricated lighting systems will come with the correct combination of tubes ready to go. All you have to do is pop them in and plug in the unit.

You must also remember that the right spectrum of light means little if the intensity is too low. While some regular-wattage fluorescent lamps come in the proper colors, they do not have a very high output at all compared with other specialized lamps. You will most certainly need high output (HO), very high output (VHO), or compact power tubes, all of which are a big step up in intensity, to keep reef aquariums, or even if you just want brighter lights. They are the most intense lights available for aquarium use by far, and they also come in a wide variety of colors, from 4,500°K all the way up to 20,000°K. However, the 5,500°K and 6,500°K varieties not only seem to be the most reliable but also are also the cheapest. When used with actinic fluorescent tubes they provide enough lighting of the right spectrum to keep any reef organisms very healthy.

Unfortunately, the brighter a particular type of light is, the more it usually costs and the more the fixtures and other associated hardware cost as well. Also, these lamps tend to change color over time. You may not notice any difference at all, but they do change spectra as they get older, and they must be replaced every year or so depending on the particular type being used. You cannot simply wait for them to burn out, as this takes several times longer than the lamp takes to change color. So keep in mind the cost of replacing all of your lights every year when deciding on a lighting system for your aquarium. Many of the more intense lighting systems will also get very hot and will require you to purchase special cooling fans that can be mounted in the canopy or fixture to help keep the temperature down. Keep this extra expense in mind as well. Again, most of these things are already taken care of in prefabricated lighting systems.

Metal halide bulbs look familiar because they are the same type as commonly used in street lighting. The 10,000 K bulb shown here is as bright as a street light but provides a different color.

When it comes to deciding how much light to put over your aquarium, just remember that for the most part you should try to fit the greatest number of lamps you can over the aquarium without causing the water to overheat and without completely breaking your wallet. It's practically impossible to overdo it.

Setting Up Your Reef Aquarium

The first thing you'll need to do when setting up your new reef aquarium is to figure out where to put it. The aquarium has to be placed on a sturdy floor that is as level as possible. Remember that water weighs over 8 pounds per gallon, so even a relatively small 30-gallon reef aquarium will weigh about 300 pounds by the time you add the weight of the tank itself, the stand, filters, rocks, and water. Make sure that you don't put it where the floor may warp or fail, letting the aquarium fall through. Also keep in mind that if the floor is not level it can lead to leaks (or worse), because a tilted aquarium places greater stress on one side. Over time this can cause the seals to become weakened or fail. Also make sure to leave enough room between the aquarium and the wall behind it for your equipment. Measure how much space will be needed for box filters, skimmers, hoses—and anything else that will hang off the back of the tank—and make the necessary adjustment in the position of the

The depth of the tank used for a marine aquarium greatly affects the intensity of the light that reaches the bottom of the aquarium. Reef invertebrates' lighting preferences have to be taken into account when they're being situated within the aquarium. Photo by Jose Reyes

aquarium. Obviously, once you fill the tank with water you probably will not be able to move it even an inch without draining some or all of the water back out of it because of the weight. And even if you *can* move it it's a bad idea to do so, as having a large volume of water sloshing around in the tank will put unnatural stresses on it.

The next step should be mixing up your synthetic sea water. You can mix it up one bucket at a time or simply mix it right in the aquarium. If you plan on using tap water (but I suggest that you don't), have it tested for any appreciable concentration of ammonia, nitrite, or nitrate. It is also a good idea to have the water tested for phosphate, the nutrient that can cause unwanted algae to grow. If your tap water has phosphate in it you will have to purchase a phosphate remover. Copper is also commonly found in tap water that runs through copper pipes. Copper is deadly to many invertebrates if concentrations are high enough. So if you find that your tap water has ammonia, nitrite, nitrate, phosphate, or copper in it you will certainly have better luck using purified or distilled water.

The salts on the market generally require about half a cupful of salt per gallon of fresh water to make salt water with a specific gravity of 1.023, which is ideal. So mix the water and synthetic salt accordingly until you have enough to almost fill the aquarium, but remember to leave enough room in the aquarium to add your live rock without causing an overflow. Also be sure to use a chlorine/chloramine remover if you decide to use tap water; these harmful chemicals must be removed or neutralized. To aid in mixing you can use a powerhead or two placed in the aquarium. Then after the water is thoroughly mixed, use a hydrometer to check that the specific gravity is between 1.021 and 1.025. If the specific gravity is higher than 1.023, add a little more fresh water; if it is lower, add a little more salt. You will eventually get the hang of this and be able to make up batches of salt water relatively quickly.

After several hours, check the pH of the aquarium's water. It should be around 8.2 at this time (between 7.9 and 8.5 is acceptable, but 8.2 is the optimum). Keep in mind that although tap water and distilled water usually have a pH much lower than 8.0, the pH should rise after synthetic salt is added. If the pH still remains low, a pH buffer may be needed to bring it up to ideal levels. Just follow the manufacturer's directions for whatever type is used.

Next you should put the filters in place whether it be in, under, or on the aquarium You should first test them to ensure that they function properly in order to correct any problems before going any further. Whatever you are using, make sure to closely follow the instructions of the manufacturer or someone you trust, such as a *knowledgeable* aquarium store employee. Also pay attention to details such as whether the filter needs to be filled with water before plugging it in or whether it is self priming. For larger scale systems in which you might employ the use of a sump tank, be sure to carefully watch any hoses or other plumbing for leaks. Even a tiny drip can lead to major problems over time and should be taken care of before going any further. Skimmers and any other accessories such as additional powerheads should also be brought into service at this time. Because there is a lack of dissolved organic compounds in the water at this point (or at least there should be), skimmers may not produce any foam at all. In fact, they may not produce any foam for several weeks to come. Keep in mind that this is perfectly normal when getting started. Just make sure that it seems to be operating correctly and isn't leaking. Also, on occasion when first starting, (or after a power outage) powerheads and other types of pumps may not work. If this happens all you should need to do is give them a good shaking or a hard pop or two on top with your fingers. They should start up and work properly or should be replaced.

If everything is running smoothly you should now be ready to hook up the lighting system. If you use a system with several fluorescent tubes or one that uses compact power

tubes you must pay special attention to the ballast box(es) that powers them. These tar-filled boxes can get extremely hot and must be placed away from the aquarium itself. Placing them under the canopy with the lamps or underneath the cabinet will almost certainly lead to the overheating of the aquarium in a short time. Instead, try to place the ballast box(es) on the floor behind or beside the cabinet or attach it as high as possible to the back of the canopy on the outside. This keeps the ballast box exposed to open air and helps to keep heat transfer to the aquarium at a minimum.

Aquariums of different sizes and types have differing circulation and pumping requirements. Fortunately, the availability of quietly operating pumps of varying capacities allows aquarists to tailor their aquariums' requirements for the energy-efficient delivery of power to the different pump sizes offered.

HO and VHO fluorescent systems may also have a tar-filled ballast that must be dealt with in the same manner. However, the more expensive systems use a lightweight non-tar electronic ballast that does not generate anywhere near the amount of heat that a tar-filled ballast does. Many electronic ballasts also have an aluminum heat sink or an internal cooling fan to help out. Nevertheless, they still generate at least some heat and should also be placed somewhere other than under the cabinet or inside the canopy. Probably the best place for them is on the back of the canopy. Systems that use metal halide bulbs have the largest ballast boxes, and as you might expect these generate quite a bit of heat as well. Again, make sure to keep these boxes out from underneath the cabinet. In most cases there will be no other option, simply because of their size, except to place them on the floor next to the aquarium. The exception here is a ballast that is mounted inside a prefabricated canopy. This is common in compact power systems and some VHO systems, but these systems without exception will also have built-in fans to cool both the lights and the ballast box.

After the lights have been on for several hours you should also check the aquarium's temperature. Usually even with fans and remote ballasts the lights will still transfer at least some heat to the aquarium. Remember that the aquarium should be around 75 degrees Fahrenheit and shouldn't ever be more than 6 to 8 degrees higher or lower. If it is much higher than 75 degrees you will need to add fans to the canopy to cool the lighting system if none are already there. If there are already fans in use, another method of lowering the temperature of the aquarium is to place a fan or fans in such a way that they blow across the surface of the aquarium and increase the rate of evaporation from the aquarium. When water evaporates from the aquarium it creates a cooling effect that can drop the temperature of the aquarium by several degrees. Unfortunately this means you'll have to keep a close watch on the water level and add replacement water more frequently. Never forget that when water evaporates from the aquarium the salt does not, so always use fresh water to replace evaporated water. The salinity of the aquarium increases as water evaporates, so replacements should be made often in order to keep the water conditions inside the aquarium as stable as possible.

In a cold house your aquarium may actually have a temperature that is too low even after the lights have been on for several hours. Or the aquarium may experience a drop in temperature at night when the lights are off. Unless you live in a tropical area, you'll need a heater. Install your heater in an area where there is good circulation so that the warmed water is moved around the aquarium. Most heaters come with a thermostat adjustment, and many have temperatures marked on them. Be careful; even the best heaters on the market may be off by several degrees. This can be the result of several factors. Most commonly it occurs simply because the heater is too small for the aquarium and cannot heat it up to the point that you set the thermostat on, even if it stays on constantly. If this happens you may have to purchase a larger heater, or even an extra heater that can be placed elsewhere in the aquarium.

It's hard to be patient, but you should let the entire system run normally for *at least* a couple of days. Make sure to run the lighting system for just as long as you normally will. Re-check the salinity and pH, and periodically check the temperature. Also re-check all hoses, fittings, and other equipment for leaks or other problems.

If you feel confident that everything is working properly, you are finally ready to start adding live rock to the aquarium, which is actually the first step in establishing a biological filter and stocking the aquarium. It sounds simple, but arranging the live rock in a suitable manner can actually be quite a task. Whether all of your live rock is relatively consistent or completely inconsistent in shape and size is irrelevant. You should try as far as possible to build the most open "framework" of rock possible. Stack the pieces randomly and in a way that provides the least amount of contact between them, which in turn should provide lots of space between the rocks. This allows better water circulation throughout the aquarium and behind the rock. Because live rock is sold by the pound it will save you money to use the smallest quantity required to make your aquarium look "full." Loosely spacing the rock will help you do

The cost of heating a mini-reef aquarium should be taken into account by anyone thinking of setting one up. Today the purchase of powerful and provably dependable aquarium heaters represents only a very small portion of the total costs involved with acquiring and stocking a mini-reef aquarium—but the cost of the electricity consumed can be an altogether different story.

Live rock should be arranged in the aquarium so that circulation through it is not impeded and no "dead" spots are created. Contact between individual pieces should be kept to a minimum— yet at the same time the construction has to be sturdy enough to keep from being toppled by any of the tank inhabitants, some of whom can be destructively clumsy.
Photo by U. Erich Friese

this. Try placing bigger pieces at the bottom with several inches of space between them, then start to stack the other pieces on top to build a wall of rock up the back of the aquarium. Your wall should start wide at the bottom then angle back toward the back of the aquarium. This gives the wall more stability and will also provide more places to put corals and other livestock which need as much light as possible. You may have to try several times with several arrangements to get it right, but try to take the time to get it the way you want it to stay before you begin adding livestock. Rearranging later, especially if you have already added corals and other invertebrates, can be very troublesome. As you stack individual pieces of live rock you should also wiggle them around a bit to make sure that they will not topple before placing any livestock on top of them.

Once you are finished building your live rock wall you should add just enough substrate to cover the bottom that is still exposed at the front of the aquarium. You don't need to put any behind the live rock, because it will only get dirty and trap detritus in places where it will be very difficult to clean. Also make sure to rinse the substrate well before putting it into the aquarium, because it can get very dusty during shipping and handling. If you don't, your aquarium will end up very cloudy and can take several days or longer to clear up.

At this point adjust the powerheads or pump returns so that they provide the greatest amount of circulation throughout the aquarium. This will also take a little trial and error. In most cases you can simply put a powerhead in each of the back corners of the aquarium and point them at the front center of the aquarium. Once you get them set where you think they do the best job you will finally be ready to move on with the process of stocking your new reef aquarium.

GETTING INTO MINI-REEFS

Stocking Your Reef Aquarium

Now that we've gone over the basics of equipment and setup we can move on to the good stuff: stocking your reef aquarium. The most common animals in the marine aquarium hobby are fish, but there are many, many other types of organisms as well that you as a reef hobbyist will be able to keep. All of these other animals collected (and now, increasingly more often, bred) for the aquarium trade are lumped under the group name "invertebrates," the presence or absence of a backbone being a handy way of separating the fish from the other animals commonly seen in an aquarium. The invertebrates include the sponges (poriferans), clams and snails (mollusks), worms (annelids in this case), crabs and shrimps (crustaceans), starfish (echinoderms), and corals, anemones, and sea fans (cnidarians). (The invertebrate label wouldn't include the sea squirts, which technically have been placed in the same phylum as the fish.) Several decorative non-vascular plants, commonly called macroalgae, are also available. Considering that there usually are several dozen members of each of these groups of fish, invertebrates, and plants, you have quite a variety of livestock to choose from. In this book everything that you will be able to keep in your aquarium can be placed into four basic categories: cnidarian invertebrates, other invertebrates, algae, and of course fish. Since you are just beginning your venture into the reef aquarium hobby only general information is given about many groups of organisms. Also keep in mind that only those organisms that are well suited to keeping by beginners—as well as, by way of warning, those that should be avoided—are discussed. There are literally hundreds of other corals, fish, sponges, shrimps, etc., that you may come across and may be more prepared to care for in the future.

There is only one more thing to discuss before you actually start to add animals to your aquarium. There is a break-in period known as "cycling" that

Some of the most interesting marine animals are, unfortunately, among the most difficult to maintain. A number of clams and snails are among the most popular of marine invertebrates, but mollusks like this squid present far too many problems. Photo by MP.and C. Piednoir, Aqua Press

you must understand in order to avoid trouble. As discussed earlier, the waters around coral reefs in nature are effectively free of ammonia. Therefore we must make sure that the concentration of ammonia in the aquarium is always zero as well. The bacteria that use ammonia as a food source must be given time to multiply within the aquarium in order to establish a biological filter, and the time that this (and the related conversion of nitrite to nitrate) takes is the "cycle."

After setting up a normal marine aquarium this wait period usually takes 3 to 5 weeks and is started by setting up the "dead" biological filter, then adding one or two small fish and nothing else to the aquarium. The fish carry some of the bacteria that will slowly begin to consume the toxins that the fish excrete. The bacteria will then multiply until an equilibrium is reached between the amount of ammonia produced by the fish and the amount consumed by the bacteria. As this equilibrium is reached the ammonia is converted into nitrite, which is also poisonous. This rise in nitrite levels brings on the growth of another type of bacterium that uses it for food instead of ammonia. So now you have to wait for these bacteria to multiply and reach an equilibrium with the amount of nitrite being produced by the ammonia-eating bacteria. After both types of bacteria are well established in the biological filter and ammonia and nitrite levels drop to zero, the cycling process is complete and more livestock can be added. The process normally takes about a month.

However, when setting up a reef aquarium you *may* be able to avoid nearly this entire process. If good live rock is added to the aquarium when it is being set up the wait period is typically much, much shorter, because the rock may already be heavily colonized with the required bacteria. The best thing to do is get the aquarium up and running, add the live rock and one or two damselfish, then wait a few days and test the water for both ammonia and nitrite. If there is even a trace of either you should wait a few more days and try again, but as soon as both reach zero you are done waiting for the cycling to finish and you can begin slowly adding more livestock.

The primary animals that are added to any reef aquarium are live corals. These corals, along with sea anemones, jellyfish, and other related animals, all belong to the biological group known as the phylum Cnidaria (pronounced ny-dar-re-ah; the "C" is silent). All are very simple invertebrates, and while many may look radically different from each other they are actually all similar in basic structure and are relatively closely related. First, all cnidarians have the same basic body construction at the tissue level of organization. All have a body wall composed of an outer layer called the ectodermis, which is comparable to the animal's "skin," and an inner layer called the endodermis. Between these two layers is a clear jelly-like material called the mesoglea. Typical cnidarians have a prominent mouth that opens into a large single body cavity. The cavity acts as

The polyps of a healthy flowerpot coral, Goniopora *sp., one of the stony corals, are fully expanded here.*

the organism's stomach and is called the gastrovascular cavity. The mouth is typically surrounded by a ring of tentacles of varying size whose primary function is to help the animal capture and eat food. To aid in this task any tentacles present are usually covered by thousands of specialized cells called cnidocytes, which are unique to the cnidarians. In fact, the name of these cells is where the whole group got its name from. These cells are commonly called nematocysts and are similar to tiny poisonous harpoons because they

This plate coral is a non-colonial cnidarian that lives as a single polyp. The centrally situated mouth can be clearly seen in the middle of the body.

can explode outward, shooting a tiny toxic barb into an attacker as a defensive measure, or into a prey organism during the capture of food. These tiny poisonous harpoons are well known in cnidarians such as stinging jellyfish and the fire corals, but very few if any cnidarians available to hobbyists carry such a powerful punch. Most cannot even give you a sting that is feelable through the thick skin on your hands.

Different cnidarians can be found as individual animals or as members of complex colonies. Each animal, as an individual or as part of a colony, is called a polyp, and each polyp has a mouth, a gastrovascular cavity, etc. Often in the colonial cnidarians each polyp can be so well integrated with the surrounding polyps that it is practically impossible to tell where one polyp stops and another starts, because they actually share a common ectodermis and mesoglea. In such cases the tissues of these cnidarians are so intimately connected that the colony lives as if it were one organism, sharing the food and nutrients taken in and produced by each individual polyp.

A closed brain coral showing tissue recession along its edge, leaving the skeleton exposed in the area in which deterioration has progressed the most.

Many cnidarians are carnivorous, eating anything from the smallest plankton to relatively large fish. Cnidarians that have relatively large tentacles often grab onto and eat anything meaty that they can get a grip on, while many others that do not

This green brain coral is suffering from tissue recession and may not survive. The coral's white skeleton is visible where the tissue is missing—which should be a clear warning to anyone thinking of purchasing this specimen.

have large tentacles (or have no obvious tentacles at all) cover themselves with a thin layer of mucus, which is used to collect bacteria and plankton as if it were fly-paper. This mucous sheet is "reeled in" to the mouth, then moved to the gastrovascular cavity, where the food particles are digested. Some cnidarians use both of these methods of feeding.

As discussed previously, many cnidarians, especially corals, also receive large amounts of nutrients from single-celled algae that live in their tissues. These tiny organisms are called zooxanthellae, and the relationship between a cnidarian host and its zooxanthellae is called a symbiosis. Like terrestrial plants, the zooxanthellae take in carbon dioxide and give off oxygen while producing food. This provides the host cnidarian animal's cells with a constant internal source of oxygen, carbohydrates, and a variety of other vital nutrients produced during photosynthesis. In return, the cnidarian provides the algae with a place to call home as well as a source of carbon dioxide, phosphate, and other nutrients.

Cnidarians that live attached to the seafloor in a reef environment must compete for growing space on the reef and must also protect themselves from predation by a variety of other organisms. Among the basic weapons that some cnidarians employ are thin digestive filaments that are normally kept inside the gastrovascular cavity. If something irritating or threatening comes into contact with particular cnidarians these filaments are spit out through the mouth and quickly begin secreting digestive substances directly onto whatever they touch, damaging or killing it. If tentacles are present they can more than likely give a competitor or attacker a sting from the nematocysts. Still other cnidarians can produce waterborne toxins. These toxic substances are released into the surrounding water, where they spread and irritate or poison other cnidarians that are too close. For these reasons it is very important to be careful which cnidarians you add to your aquarium and where you place them as well. In general it is best to simply choose less "aggressive" cnidarians or make sure that you don't place any of them in direct contact with each other, or even very near each other. In fact, it is best in the beginning to always

This staghorn coral has suffered a partial bleaching of its tissue and should be passed over for purchase.

GETTING INTO MINI-REEFS

leave at least a few inches between all specimens until you can figure out who can touch whom without doing any damage.

There are a few things that you should always take into consideration when shopping for cnidarians. First are the obvious things to think about. Is it too big for your aquarium? Will its tentacles reach out and kill everything in your aquarium? Are your lights bright enough to keep it healthy?, etc. Next are a few other things to look out for that may not seem so straightforward or easily recognized. Never buy any type of cnidarian that has any kind of tissue damage or decay or is suffering from tissue recession. This is usually seen as areas of the body that have a moldy or rotten look to them. Dead or damaged flesh is often covered by a nasty brown jelly-like material, while in other cases it is only evident as obvious areas missing flesh where the animal's skeleton (if present) shows prominently. This condition usually worsens over a short period of time and can lead to the death of an individual or sometimes a whole colony. You should also avoid any type of cnidarian that has "bleached." This is a condition in which the cnidarian has lost most or all of its zooxanthellae and has turned white or almost clear. This is a common side effect of the animal's getting too hot during shipping, but it can also be caused by other factors, such as lack of intense light or exposure to excessive UV radiation. Also avoid cnidarians that are not "polyped out" or expanded. Most cnidarians absorb water into their tissues during the day and swell up and/or extend numerous tiny polyps. Likewise, most all retract somewhat at night or when they are irritated or unhealthy. Most corals will be shrunken and

A healthy coral will normally expand its polyps during the day. The small toadstool leather coral above, for example, has all of its polyps fully expanded and appears to be doing well, whereas the similar toadstool coral below has all of its polyps retracted and may be having trouble. Almost every coral will keep its polyps retracted at least some of the time, but a coral's staying closed up for more than a couple of days in a row almost certainly indicates trouble.

retracted when they arrive at a store, but if they are healthy they should begin to expand within a couple of days at most. If after a few days a specimen has not at least begun to expand it should not be purchased. Good common sense is one of the most valuable tools you can use when making selections. Don't push your luck trying to add things that you know may not be wise choices. You may pay dearly in the end.

This oddly shaped leather coral has completely bleached out and will not survive.

STONY, OR HARD, CORALS

The first group of cnidarians to discuss is the stony corals, also called hard corals. They are placed taxonomically within the phylum Cnidaria in the class Anthozoa, subclass Zoantharia, order Scleractinia. These stony corals produce a hard white skeleton made of calcium carbonate in the form of the mineral aragonite. These skeletons can be almost entirely exposed in some groups or completely covered with flesh in other groups. As discussed, they can also be found as individual animals or polyps and in colonies over ten feet across that comprise thousands upon thousands of polyps. As far as care in the aquarium goes, no matter the type or size, they will all need bright light and will also require additives. Stony corals require the addition of calcium, strontium, and iodine on a regular basis. They also require that you maintain a high alkalinity and low phosphate level.

When choosing stony corals make sure to look for any tissue damage, and also look closely for areas of tissue recession, which are seen as areas where the coral's body has pulled away from the skeleton. This is usually very obvious, because the coral's white skeleton shows prominently. You should also avoid any stony coral whose skeleton shows obvious breakage, because where there is broken skeleton there is usually torn flesh. If this is the case the coral may later succumb to complications from tissue decay or recession.

Of all of the stony corals to choose from, the GREEN OPEN BRAIN CORALS and RED OPEN BRAIN CORALS (*Trachyphyllia geoffroyi*--both are actually the same species) are probably the best to start with. They are definitely one of the most popular and readily available stony corals. Their name comes from their resemblance to a small colorful brain when they are fully expanded; they are usually iridescent combinations of green and red. Both of these brain corals are very large individual polyps with cone-shaped skeletons that usually start as ovals and then take on a figure-eight shape as the corals grow, almost always having the same characteristic shape. Both will thrive under moderate to intense

The photo above shows what the aragonite skeleton of a common brain coral looks like after the coral has died and the flesh has rotted away. The photo below shows a similar coral that is alive and well. It is easy to see that many corals are predominately skeletons with just a rind of flesh covering them.

*An open brain coral (*Trachyphyllia geoffroyi *in this case) showing the typical figure-eight configuration of this species. This specimen is red, but green individuals of the same species are available also.*

lighting but will also tolerate lower light levels in aquariums that have several fluorescent tubes rather than a few high-output lamps. They also do well with a light to moderate current, and they tend to be exceptionally hardy. Their fleshy bodies expand well beyond their skeletons; they have very small tentacles that typically are extended at night or when eating, but they lack long stinging tentacles and can be placed very near other corals without much risk of trouble.

TOOTH CORALS, also called flat brain corals and lobo brain corals (*Lobophyllia* spp.), are named for the large tooth-like projections and ridges on their skeletons that can often be seen through the fleshy body. These corals too are considered by most to be open brain corals, but they come in several shapes, sizes, and colors. They are most commonly green, brown, or red but may also be purple, pink, blue, or other colors as well. Tooth corals can take on a shape very similar to that of the red and green brains, and they can also take on a branching shape that gives rise to several individual polyps. All will do well under moderate to intense lighting but can also tolerate lower light conditions. They also do well with a light to moderate current, and all tend to be very hardy. They have very short feeding tentacles that are extended at night, but none have dangerous tentacles; like other brains, they can be placed very near other corals.

BUTTON CORALS (*Scolymia* spp. and *Cynarina* spp.), also called doughnut corals, are close relatives of the brain and tooth corals. These corals, however, do not have much of a variety of skeletal shapes. They are all relatively round (hence their names of button and doughnut), and the two can be very difficult to tell apart. Many *Cynarina* have swollen translucent bodies that look very fragile, while most *Scolymia* have much thicker, tougher-looking flesh, but there are other varieties that fall in between. They also come in a variety of colors from deep red to brown and green, all of which will do well under moderate to intense lighting and will live under lower light conditions. Like their cousins they will do best with a light to moderate current, tend to be very hardy, and can be placed very near other corals.

Above: A common tooth coral, also called lobo brain coral. Below: a tooth coral with a branched skeleton instead of the more usual solid skeleton of the open brain corals. One of the polyps of this colony has died, and its skeleton is exposed to show the jagged skeletal ridges that give this coral its common name.

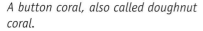

A button coral, also called doughnut coral.

The ELEGANCE CORAL (*Cataphyllia jardinei*), also called meat coral, is another good stony coral for the beginner. Elegance corals are large solitary corals that are usually quite hardy and do very well in aquariums if they survive shipping without any tissue damage. In fact, under optimal conditions elegance corals will often expand to a much larger size in an aquarium than they do in the wild. Their beautiful tentacles are usually fully extended during the day, and the coral is usually a combination of green, gray, pink, brown, or purple and is very fleshy (hence the name meat coral). They all will do well under moderate to intense lighting, but like the open brains they can also tolerate lower light conditions, often being found in cloudier waters in the wild. They also prefer a low to moderate current in which they can fully expand. Unfortunately, they are also one of the few corals that can actually give you an annoying sting on the hand if not carefully handled by the skeleton. For

All three of the button corals shown on this page are very closely related, yet each looks distinctive. Their colors and degrees of expansion—as well as other superficial characteristics—are highly variable, and it is very difficult to identify them as to genus much less to species.

As different as these corals look, it is hard to believe that they are of the same species: they both are elegance corals, Catalaphyllia jardinei. *Elegance corals can be found in many shapes and sizes and also in many different colors.*

While this coral looks very similar to a short-tentacle plate coral, it is actually a long-tentacle plate coral that has its tentacles retracted. These corals commonly retract their tentacles in the dark and then re-extend them when the light returns. Some other hard corals do exactly the opposite

this reason they should always be given a few inches of space so that their tentacles cannot come into contact with other cnidarians in your aquarium.

PLATE CORALS are another good choice. They come in two basic varieties, the short-tentacle plate (*Fungia* spp. and *Cycloseris* spp.) and the long-tentacle plate (*Heliofungia* spp.) both of which have a relatively flat circular skeleton that is completely enveloped in flesh and covered by numerous ridges. Obviously the short-tentacled variety has a body that is covered with very short tentacles (if any are actually present at all), and the long-tentacled variety is covered with long tentacles, sometimes reaching lengths of over 6 inches, giving it an appearance similar to that of a sea anemone. Each individual plate coral is actually one very large

This is what a long-tentacle plate coral (Heliofungia *sp. shown here) looks like with its tentacles expanded. It's easy to see why these coral are often mistaken for anemones!*

polyp with a large centrally located mouth, and most will do well under a wide range of lighting conditions; they are not too picky about current, either, as long as it doesn't blow them away. They are very hardy, their only particular requirement being that they be placed flat on the bottom of the aquarium with enough space to stretch out their tentacles.

The TONGUE CORALS (*Herpolitha* spp.) and SLIPPER CORALS (*Polyphyllia* spp.) also are hardy corals that are well suited to the beginner. Tongue corals look just like a big hairy tongue, and slipper corals supposedly look something like a fuzzy house slipper. The only noticeable difference in the two is the long groove that runs down the middle of a tongue coral's body, making it look even more like what it is called. Like the plate corals, tongue and slipper corals do well

This common short-tentacle plate coral is in the genus Fungia.

*This slipper coral (*Polyphyllia *sp.) may not look much like any slipper you might have seen—but the common names for many of the other corals are not really any more usefully descriptive, either.*

The small hole in the flesh near the center of this deteriorating flowerpot coral's side reveals the coral's skeleton, indicating a tissue recession that will get progressively worse, eventually killing the whole colony.

under most any lighting conditions and currents; like the plate corals, they should always be placed flat on the bottom of the aquarium.

Again, these are just a few of the corals that will prove to be hardy varieties. Notice that there is a common thread running through these hardy types: they all have large fleshy bodies and can tolerate variable conditions. Unlike these few suggestions, there are also types of corals to mention that may be popular and even hardy but are still not good choices for the hobbyist who is just getting started. In general it is a good idea to stay away from any corals that have very small polyps such as those of the genus *Acropora* (usually called SPSs—small-polyped stony corals). These corals require intense lighting and exceptional water quality to thrive and are also among the most expensive corals, which can hurt your wallet substantially if they are lost. You should also be wary of corals that have specialized stinging tentacles called "sweepers." These sweepers are tentacles that can be extended out to several times the length of the "normal" tentacles and are used to injure neighbors. For obvious reasons you should avoid them until you have a good idea of exactly how you want to arrange your corals and you are prepared to reserve a large enough space in the aquarium for them to expand fully without coming into any contact with other corals. This includes HAMMER and FROGSPAWN corals (*Euphyllia* spp.), GALAXY or CRYSTAL corals (*Galaxea* spp.), HORN CORALS (*Hydnophora* spp.), and a few others. You should

An Acropora *species with its polyps emerging at night.* Acropora *and other small-polyped stony corals are in general more difficult to keep than the large-polyped corals.* Photo by Walt Deas

make sure to ask about them at the store before you make any purchase.

One other stony coral in particular should be mentioned here, the FLOWERPOT CORAL (*Goniopora* spp.). These corals are some of the most beautiful available, but almost without exception they will not live more than a few months in aquariums. The reason why is not clear, but these corals tend to suffer from a slow but persistent loss of tissue until they die. They are regularly offered for sale, but hobbyists' continued lack of success with them indicates that they probably shouldn't be.

SOFT CORALS, LEATHER CORALS

There are several kinds of cnidarians that, unlike the stony corals, do not build any type of hard skeleton. They are grouped within the two subclasses and a number of different orders within the class Anthozoa. In the aquarium hobby the most important of these cnidarians are those that are included in the order Alcyonacea of the subclass Alcyonaria. This order contains the cnidarians usually referred to as "soft" corals, even though many of them, while lacking any rigid skeleton, still

This frogspawn coral and many others have specialized tentacles called "sweepers," which can be extended to several times normal tentacle length. They can stretch out—at times up to six inches—and sting anything within reach.

*The beautiful polyps of a healthy and fully expanded flowerpot coral (*Goniopora *sp.) make it easy to see why flowerpot corals are among hobbyists' favorites.*

tend to be somewhat tough in texture. These tough-textured cnidarians feel to the human touch much like leather and are thus called leather corals by hobbyists. The others have a much softer feel and are somewhat "squishy" to the touch; they tend to be called soft corals. The situation is somewhat confused by the tendency within the aquarium trade to use the term "soft corals" much more broadly, in reference to almost every anthozoan except the scleractinian corals (the hard, or stony, corals.) Both leather corals and soft corals are on average much hardier than the stony corals and are easier to care for, and in many aquariums they can grow so much that they have to be periodically pruned like shrubs.

These corals are covered with polyps that have eight tentacles (as differentiated from the hard corals and other cnidarians of the subclass Zoantharia, whose tentacles are

A toadstool leather coral of the genus Sarcophyton.

A finger leather coral of the genus Sinularia. *Finger leathers come in a wide variety of shapes, sizes, and colors, from short and fat with thick branches to tall and skinny with thin branches.*

Both photos show Sarcophyton *toadstool leather corals. Notice the slightly different shape of the main body of each coral and the variable shape and size of the polyps that are extended during the day.*

This finger leather coral is in the process of shedding a wax coat that has covered the entire coral for three days.

arranged in groups and multiples of six) that in many cases are pinnate, meaning the tentacles themselves are covered with smaller tentacles. The expansion of the polyps is commonly called "polyping out" by hobbyists and is easy to observe as the corals react to the aquarium's lights being turned on in the morning. It is common to see these polyps fully expanded during the day and then completely retracted into little pores at night.

Both the leather corals and the soft corals contain zooxanthellae and do not require any sort of feeding. Of course this means they will need strong lighting in order to thrive and grow. Some types can grow several inches in one year if kept under very intense lighting. Fortunately, many will also live under lower lighting conditions as well; they just might not grow. About the only additive that they require is some source of iodine, which should be added on a regular basis to ensure that your specimens will stay healthy.

Many of these corals use various chemicals to weaken other nearby corals and inhibit their growth. These toxins can have a very strong effect on corals within a few inches, but can also have lessened yet noticeable negative effects on corals farther away if they are down-current. In this case, the coral producing the toxin is giving the down-current coral a weak but constant bath of poison. If you suspect this is happening in your aquarium, try to move corals around to different locations and always make sure that any leather or other soft coral is placed in an area with good circulation.

When shopping for leather or soft corals you should pay attention to whether or not the coral is well expanded. If a coral keeps its polyps retracted for more than a day or two, it may be unhealthy and should be avoided. If you find a healthy one and it will not expand in your aquarium, the lack of expansion may be the result of the coral's placement, as mentioned above. Just try to move it a time or two and see whether you get better results.

Many leather corals produce a waxy coating over their bodies, but this is normal. This coating usually covers most of the coral but is especially thick upon the top of leather corals that have flattened or cup-shaped upper bodies. The coating is eventually sloughed away

Above: A Sarcophyton *toadstool leather coral showing one of the variable shapes in this group. Right: A finger leather coral,* Sinularia *species.*

One of the Sinularia *species of finger leather corals showing the thick-branched short form taken by some finger leathers.*

after a few days, and it is thought that this is a mechanism for allowing the coral to remove any unwanted material that has settled or grown on it. While in most cases this seems to be a harmless process, on occasion it has been observed that the wax can strongly irritate other corals that it may come to rest upon in the aquarium. So it is a good idea to watch closely if a leather coral begins to shed its wax coat and remove any bits and pieces that you can. A leather coral's failure to shed its coat within a few days may be a sign that the coral is irritated and may require being moved.

A typical lettuce coral (Lobophytum sp.). It has very few polyps on its body, which is normal for this type of coral; some lettuce corals show none.

Most of the leather corals are quite hardy and will do well. The most common types are the toadstool

A colt coral (Cladiella sp.), one of the most popular and fastest-growing of all alcyonaceans.

leather corals (*Sarcophyton* spp.), finger leather corals (*Sinularia* spp.), and lettuce corals (*Lobophytum* spp.). As the name implies, toadstool leather corals have a shape that looks like a toadstool mushroom; they are usually covered with numerous thin-stalked polyps that look like tiny flowers. Finger leather corals take on a branching fingered form much like some kind of thick-stemmed plant and have short, almost fuzzy polyps. Lettuce corals have a folded sheet-like form that looks like thick lettuce leaves, but they tend to have only a few very small polyps. Another popular soft coral is the colt coral (*Cladiella* spp.). It's not clear where the name comes from, but these beautiful corals have lots and lots of feathery polyps and make a great addition to any

The type of xenia most commonly seen in aquarium stores; its polyps often will "pulse" as if they are waving or flashing. Unfortunately, it is impossible to determine whether the coral will pulse this way after it is moved to your aquarium. Many times the polyps, for unknown reasons, stop pulsing and never start again.

A colony of what is commonly called pom-pom xenias, showing the groups of waving polyps atop stubby branches.

aquarium. The soft corals of the genus *Xenia* (zee-nee-ah) are very popular and are highly suitable for reef aquariums. These animals come in colonies that encrust rocks much as the star polyps do, but they have long stalks and tentacles. Under strong illumination all xenia types grow relatively quickly and will spread over large areas of live rock. The colonies will also grow best when exposed to a moderate or even a strong current, making the polyps sway around. Like many other related cnidarians, the xenias do not require separate feeding, deriving all their nutrients from the water itself and their zooxanthellae, but they will thrive only if iodine is provided in sufficient quantity. In fact, if iodine levels drop too low for too long, entire colonies will die simultaneously in what most hobbyists call a "crash." Xenias are notorious for this; don't let it happen to you.

A colony of xenias that don't belong to the genus Xenia. *This large-polyped colony belongs to the genus* Anthelia *but nevertheless is usually called xenia by many hobbyists.*

One of the numerous sea fans available to hobbyists. These animals can be found in a wider variety of shapes and sizes and colors than any other cnidarians seen in the hobby.

SEA FANS AND SEA WHIPS

Sea fans and whips are also commonly called gorgonians by hobbyists; they belong to the order Gorgonacea, another of the orders in the subclass Alcyonaria. These relatives of the true corals are also colonial cnidarians, but their structure is somewhat different from that of the others. Each gorgonian consists of hundreds or thousands of polyps that produce a branching skeleton composed of a protein called gorgonin; they can grow to sizes of several feet. This skeleton is exceptionally tough yet somewhat flexible and is wrapped in flesh that varies greatly in color and thickness. The overall shape of a gorgonian can range from a finely branching plume-like form to a flattened almost mesh-like form, and on each type the polyps are found to line the entire surface of the branches. The whole of the colony

Close-up of the beautiful pinnate polyps of a typical sea whip. The fine polyps cover the entire surface of all of the sea whip's branches.

is firmly attached to the substrate by a large sturdy base composed of gorgonin. These bases are nearly impossible to detach, which is why almost all gorgonians are sold already attached to the piece of live rock they were collected on.

Gorgonians can be placed about anywhere in an aquarium where there is a constant moderate to strong current of water passing over their bodies. They do not seem to exude any toxic substances that irritate nearby neighbors and do not possess any type of venomous tentacles. However, they should not be placed where stony corals or anemones can give them a sting. They are filter feeders that capture tiny floating plankton; most are also photosynthetic and will require moderate to intense lighting to thrive. However, while the photosynthetic varieties have colored polyps, a few available species have colorless or white polyps, indicating a lack of zooxanthellae and allowing them to be kept under just about any lighting conditions.

As you shop for a gorgonian, be sure to inspect it for any obvious damage and also take a

For their own protection, gorgonians should be situated within the aquarium in places in which they are not in danger of being stung by other cnidarians.

This bubble-tip anemone, Entacmaea quadricolor, *is playing host to one of the clownfish of the genus* Amphiprion. *The interaction between sea anemones and clownfish is one of the most fascinating sights available to saltwater aquarium hobbyists—but it's not always easy to achieve, as the keeping of sea anemones presents a number of problems, one of which is their capacity to sting and kill other cnidarians.*

close look to see whether any of its skeleton is exposed. The skeleton will have a brown or black color and should not be visible if the gorgonian is completely healthy. If it is exposed anywhere it is an indication that some area of the gorgonian's tissue has died and sloughed away. Gorgonians should never be exposed to air and commonly will suffer from tissue loss or even death if they are. To avoid this, make sure that any gorgonian you purchase is put into a bag that is full of water. There should be no air in it at all. Then, when placing the specimen in your aquarium, put the whole bag into the water and open it below the surface so that the gorgonian can be removed without risk.

Unfortunately, some gorgonians tend to be only moderately hardy at best even if specimens are handled correctly and given the right conditions in the aquarium. It seems that while the gorgonians with thick fleshy branches do rather well, those with thin branches and less flesh commonly live happily for several months or even a couple of years but then wither away and die. So the thick-branched types are good choices, but others may not be.

SEA ANEMONES

Sea anemones are some of the best-known cousins of the corals. They resemble overturned jellyfish that have attached to the bottom, none having any sort of skeleton but almost all having tentacles that pack a strong sting. These tentacles can range in size from little bumps that cover the entire surface of the anemone to tentacles

GETTING INTO MINI-REEFS

that can be over 6 inches in length. These tentacles give the anemones the ability to capture prey as small as plankton or as large as fish. In fact, anemones will take all sorts of prepared foods given to them, including bits of clam and shrimp meat, and many large anemones will even take live goldfish or minnows. If they are fed such foods they will grow very quickly and reach full size in a short time. Taxonomically, the anemones are in the order Actiniaria, within the same subclass as the hard corals.

Anemones can easily be the most fascinating animals in the aquarium if they form a "bond" with certain fish. They can form unique relationships with the clownfish of the genera *Amphiprion* and *Premnas* and provide the fish with a protective shelter. This is possible because the clownfish are immune to the anemone's sting, while any predator that attempts to bother the clownfish is not. In return for this protection the clownfish will feed the anemone by collecting bits of food and placing them in the anemone's tentacles. This can be observed in aquariums if small pieces of meat are dropped into the water near an anemone that is hosting these fish.

Like many of their kin, anemones will do best under intense lighting but will survive at lower lighting intensities. However, there is one problem that must be dealt with. Anemones have a bad habit of crawling around the aquarium looking for a spot that they like instead of staying where you put them. They also tend to sting everything they touch in the process. For this reason it is best to add an anemone to the aquarium first and let it crawl anywhere it wants until it settles into a place. Usually once they pick a spot they will become firmly attached and will not move again unless you change the conditions in the aquarium (such as moving powerheads and changing the currents).

One of the most common anemones available is the bubble-tip or bulb anemone (*Entacmaea quadricolor*). These anemones are usually six inches or so in diameter and are

This common long-tentacle anemone, Macrodactyla doreensis, *is irritating the toadstool leather coral just in front of it. One of the two animals will have to be repositioned in the aquarium.*

Above: This large carpet anemone, Stichodactyla gigantea, *is providing shelter for an individual* Amphiprion clarkii. *Below: A nice condylactis anemone,* Condylactis gigantea—*an attractive species, but not one that will serve as a host to anemonefishes*

Some anemones, far from playing host to various fish species, are freeloaders on other marine animals. Here the anemone Sagartia parasitica *is going along for the ride on the back of the hermit crab* Dardanus arrosor. *Photo by MP. and C. Piednoir, Aqua Press*

covered with tentacles that are a half inch to two or three inches in length. The tentacles also typically have small bubble-like swellings near their tips, giving the anemone its name. Bubble-tip anemones will play host to several types of clownfish, including the percula clownfish (*Amphiprion percula*), the maroon clownfish (*Premnas biaculeatus*), the tomato clownfish (*Amphiprion frenatus*), the fire clownfish (*Amphiprion ephippium*), and the clarkii clownfish (*Amphiprion clarkii*, which is commonly but improperly called the sebae clownfish).

The long-tentacled anemone (*Macrodactyla doreensis*) is another popular variety. This is a very hardy and relatively large anemone, with individuals commonly reaching a diameter of twelve to eighteen inches across the disc. The tentacles are also large, reaching lengths of five to eight inches. Also, like many other anemones, the long- tentacled anemone can be found in a variety of different colors; some are even striped. Long-tentacled anemones also will play host to a few different clownfish. These include the skunk clownfish (*Amphiprion perideraion*) and the clarkii clownfish, and while it is less common they will occasionally be occupied by the maroon clownfish.

The carpet and saddle anemones (*Stichodactyla gigantea* and *Stichodactyla haddoni*, respectively) are commonly available. Both can also grow to very large sizes, often reaching a diameter of over a foot. Both have a large flattened body that can either lie flat over the substrate or fold up in a shape that resembles a saddle covered with very short tentacles. Carpet anemones will play host to several types of popular clownfish. These include the clarkii clownfish, the skunk clownfish , and the percula clownfish (*Amphiprion percula* and *Amphiprion ocellaris*, both look-alike species being referred to under the same common name) as well as several others. Saddle anemones, on the other hand, will not play host to the percula clownfish or skunk clownfish but will host the saddleback clownfish (*Amphiprion polymnus*) and sebae clownfish (*Amphiprion sebae*) as well as a few others.

Probably the most popular anemone that will not host any clownfish is the condy or condylactis anemone (*Condylactis gigantea*). This is because this anemone is found in the Caribbean Sea and other places in the Atlantic, but no clownfish are. Clowns simply have never seen these anemones and almost without exception will not go near them. But they still look great and are by far the cheapest of the anemones, so you may want to try one anyway.

MUSHROOM ANEMONES

Mushroom anemones are solitary polyps that are very similar to both the sea anemones and the stony corals, sharing characteristics with both. They are in the same subclass but in the order Corallimopharia. Of all the cnidarians available to hobbyists, the mushroom anemones may be the easiest to care for, because even though they all contain zooxanthellae, most will tolerate much lower lighting levels than other photosynthetic cnidarians. In fact, many will do fine in what would be considered the darkest parts of any reef aquarium, where they are shaded or receive only indirect light. Many types actually prefer lower light levels and will shrink up if exposed to intense lights such as metal halides. Like many other cnidarians, they assimilate all the nutrients they require from their zooxanthellae, by absorbing them directly from sea water, and by eating bacteria, so there is no need for any sort of feeding. However, a good iodine supplement should be added on a regular basis; it seems to help them grow to larger sizes more quickly.

One of the things that makes mushroom anemones among the easiest of all of the cnidarians to care for is the fact that they are for the most part very undemanding in their lighting requirements, which gives their owners great leeway in situating them within the aquarium.

The three photos on this page represent just a few of the many different types of mushroom anemones available to hobbyists. At top is an Actinodiscus *species and at bottom is a* Rhodactis *species; the mushroom anemone at center has not been identified definitively at the generic level but probably is an* Actinodiscus.

Most of the mushrooms are completely harmless, but others can be quite deadly. Just like corals or sea anemones, those that have tentacles can deliver a strong sting to other animals that are nearby, and a few others that have no tentacles at all still seem to burn other corals they come into direct contact with. You should keep a close watch on a colony of mushrooms for a while if they are placed very near other inhabitants to see whether they need to be moved.

BUTTON POLYPS AND SEA MATS

The button polyps and sea mats are very common in reef aquariums and are some of the hardiest cnidarians available to hobbyists. They are usually only a quarter of an inch to one inch in size and are secured firmly to the bottom by a fleshy base. Unlike many other cnidarians, even the largest button polyps reach a size of only a couple of inches in length. At times some of the various species have polyps that live as solitary animals, but most types are found in small clusters attached together by a common base or by thin strands of flesh typically forming large encrusting colonies that overgrow rocks and other hard surfaces on the reef.

The order Zoanthidea contains the button polyps and sea mats, among the smallest of the cnidarians regularly offered for sale and also among the ones that do best in the home aquarium. These Zoanthus *appear to be vibrantly healthy.*

All of the button polyps and sea mats have symbiotic zooxanthellae and will grow and reproduce under moderate to intense lighting, requiring only iodine as an additive. Button polyps and sea mats are not aggressive toward their neighbors, and while they do have short tentacles they do not seem to have any ability to sting. They will spread over live rock in the reef aquarium and can grow in direct contact with most other corals.

STAR POLYPS

Another group of common cnidarians that are suitable for beginners are the star polyps (*Clavularia* sp.). Star polyps are very hardy; they form colonies of closely spaced polyps and are never found as solitary individuals. The common base of attachment that they share is somewhat rubbery in texture and spreads over

Above: A group of Palythoa *button polyps. The* Palythoa *species generally are larger than the other zoanthids, reaching up to a few inches in diameter. Below: This is how a colony of star polyps looks when lights suddenly come on or when it is disturbed. All of the polyps have withdrawn into their rubbery base.*

*Below left: A small colony of star polyps (*Clavularia *sp.), one of the most beautiful of the cnidarians when viewed under strong actinic lighting; they can glow so brightly that they look as if they're giving off their own light. Below right: Less impressive but still attractive star polyps, shown taking over a large portion of previously exposed live rock in an aquarium.*

An orange sponge of the type usually referred to as a "finger" sponge because of the resemblance of its branches to pointing fingers.

rocks in an encrusting manner. Star polyps also have the ability to completely withdraw into their base. The polyps can quickly pull themselves in, looking like rapidly deflating balloons if they are disturbed or are irritated, and all that can be seen of them when withdrawn are small pimples on the surface of the base. All star polyps contain zooxanthellae and will grow best under moderate to intense lighting, and like many of their cousins they will also fare well in the aquarium only if regular additions of an iodine supplement are provided. The star polyps are in the order Stolonifera, which also contains the organ pipe corals, genus *Tubipora*.

OTHER INVERTEBRATES AND PLANTS

Now that we've discussed a variety of cnidarian invertebrates we can move on to the other types of invertebrates commonly available to hobbyists. They are very diverse groups and are lumped together here only because they all lack backbones.

Sponges

Almost any live sponge that you can find is suitable for a reef aquarium. The only problem is that most do not fare well during collection and transportation and slowly die. That is because they cannot tolerate being exposed to air. If you can find a healthy-looking sponge that doesn't have any obvious dead spots or areas, then it may be okay. Just make sure it is packed in plenty of water and that it stays submerged all the way to its new home.

Worms

Some desirable worms, including the feather duster worms and Christmas tree worms, can readily be found. Some feather duster worms live in long, thin tubes that they build by secreting a tough skin-like substance. The tubes are usually formed in the gravel or on the underside of rocks, and from the tubes the worms stick out their "dusters" into the current. This feathery body part is actually the worm's gills, which are also used to catch food as water flows through them. The Christmas tree worms are very similar, but they form hard carbonate tubes on surfaces, and their gills are shaped like a little Christmas tree instead of a duster. Of the two, the larger feather dusters will live much longer. The Christmas tree worms usually die after a few months in an aquarium.

There is one type of worm that should be avoided at all costs: the bristle, or fire, worm. These segmented worms can grow to be a few inches long—and they get that big by eating corals and gorgonians! They also have hundreds of tiny spines along their backs that can penetrate skin and be quite painful, hence the name fire worm. They are commonly found hiding in live rock and are inadvertently placed into the aquarium, where they will usually hide all day and come out only at night to feed. If you should accidentally get one of these worms in your aquarium you must trap it and remove it. Traps can be bought, but in many cases you will end up getting up at 2 in the morning with a flashlight and looking for the thing, then trapping it with a jar. This is an excellent reason to thoroughly check live rock before adding it to your aquarium.

Hermit Crabs and Shrimps

For the most part any type of hermit crab or shrimp that is for sale is suitable to put into your reef aquarium. Hermit crabs are especially valuable, for a couple of reasons. Some, such as the red-leg hermit, because they are great scavengers that roam around picking up any left-over food. The only problem that

This is a bristle worm, one of the marine aquarist's worst enemies. Usually nocturnal, these worms are hard to spot, but if you see one you'll have to get it out of the tank—which is unfortunately not always an easy job. Many bristle worms eat cnidarians of different types.

Spirobranchus giganteus, *one of the colorful and delicately shaped annelids known as Christmas tree worms.* Photo by Cathy Church

A red-leg hermit crab, Dardanus megisto. *While not as commonly seen as brown-legs and other hermit crabs, it is far more colorful.*

Above: Blue-leg hermit crabs, Paguristes sp. *Thse crabs will stay very small, but they are very good at cleaning up algae when employed in sufficient number. Below: A large banded coral shrimp,* Stenopus hispidus. Stenopus *can get to be much larger than other shrimps and are often seen trying to catch fish that come too close—fortunately, they almost never succeed. Banded coral shrimps are good scavengers and—unlike many other shrimp species—will usually walk all over the aquarium in full view.*

some crabs such as this type may present is a tendency to get big. They can grow to a couple of inches across and have a habit of knocking things over in the aquarium. Others, like blue-leg hermits and scarlet hermits, are great algae eaters and continually pick rocks clean. They also stay tiny. Other types of crabs (non-hermits) tend to be more carnivorous in nature and are best left out of reef aquariums. Many will eat coral polyps, snails, worms, etc., and even small fish if they get the chance. This is also true of the popular arrow crab. They are fine as long as you don't have any really small fish that they can grab with their pincers or any other crustaceans that they can overpower.

A few shrimps are among the other crustaceans commonly available for reef aquariums. They include the peppermint shrimp, blood shrimp, banded coral shrimp, and skunk shrimp. You generally can add several shrimp of the same species to your aquarium, with the exception of the banded coral shrimp, which will not tolerate others of its species. Of all these, the skunk shrimp, or skunk cleaner, is most desirable. These shrimp are "cleaners" that will meticulously pick parasites and dead skin off fish. The fish know what the shrimp does for them, and you can watch them come up and offer themselves for grooming. On rare occasions you may even get to see a cleaner shrimp climb onto a larger fish and go for a ride around the aquarium!

Brittle stars like this usually hide away until the aquarium lights go out, then come out to forage for leftovers.

Brittle Stars

Ophiuroid starfish of different types are relatively popular reef aquarium inhabitants. Some species will crawl around the aquarium making themselves plainly visible, but most will hide the majority of the time and can only be spotted occasionally, usually at feeding time. Many of these echinoderms, the long-armed serpent or brittle stars, have a keen sense of smell (even though they don't have a nose). When food is added they will come crawling out from their hiding places waving their arms around and trying to catch bits of food. During the rest of the day and night they slink around scavenging and cleaning the gravel of anything they can eat. If there is anything specific to remember about them it is their over-sensitivity to salinity changes. If you purchase one you must acclimate it as if it were a fish so that it is not shocked by any difference in salinity between your aquarium and the store's tanks.

Snails

Snails are sold for algae control almost exclusively. The astrea and turbo snails available to hobbyists are superb grazers that will crawl all over everything in the aquarium eating nuisance microalgae. Fortunately they do not have a taste for the desirable macroalgae that you may want to keep alive. Any reef aquarium will benefit from the addition of these little mollusks; it has even been suggested by many that you should add at least one snail for every 5 gallons of water in your aquarium.

The colorful mantles of tridacnid clams have made them popular with reef tank hobbyists; the species shown is Tridacna crocea.

Above: Astraea tecta, *because of its smaller size even more desirable than turbo snails, which can get so big that they have a tendency to knock things over during their ramblings around the aquarium. Below: A cap shell, or keyhole limpet (*Diodora sp.*), a good grazer but not often offered for sale; cap shells usually come in as hitchhikers on live rock.*

Caulerpa sertularoides, *one of the macroalgae species often available in the marine aquarium trade.*

Clams

Oftentimes quality live rock will have a variety of small clams already attached to it when purchased. These hitchhikers are fine as long as they don't die and foul the water once you place them into your aquarium. Check clams that are on live rock simply by giving them a good sniff. If they have died you will know it immediately. Once they're in the aquarium you should keep an eye on them to make sure they stay alive. Many will gape open if they are dead or will not shut quickly when bothered if they are in poor health.

Other clams popular with hobbyist are the tridacnids. These relatively large mollusks share a common feature with many cnidarians in that they contain zooxanthellae. These clams actually gape open all day and extend a thin fleshy mantle out of the shell in order to catch sunlight. The flesh can come in an almost endless variety of colors and patterns, and the clams can rival any coral in beauty. Unfortunately they are expensive, and many tend not to be particularly hardy, so be sure to give a tridacnid clam a quick check before making a purchase. The clams should gape open all day, with their mantles extended well outside of the shell if they are healthy. They also should react quickly to a shadow passing over them. They have tiny eyespots that detect rapid changes in overhead light (which could be the overhead passing of a fish on the reef). Simply wave your hand over the clam to make an overhead shadow and see whether it reacts by trying to quickly close up its shell. If it just sits there it is probably in poor health.

Macroalgae

Macroalgae is a term that generally applies to all of the desirable types of large algae that will grow in an aquarium. There are quite a few different types, but the most commonly available are several species of *Caulerpa*. These algae can have a wide variety of forms, from grape-like to fern-like, but all are very simple plants. All will usually do well, and in some cases they can actually do too well. Some caulerpas will grow so fast that they have to be pruned every few days to keep them from overgrowing corals and other aquarium inhabitants.

Other algae can actually precipitate a hard skeleton. Coralline algae produce a thin carbonate crust all over the rocks and glass of a healthy aquarium, giving it a pink, red, or purple color. Calcareous algae, such as *Halimeda*, on the other hand, can produce a segmented upright branching structure.

FISH

The most important thing to take into consideration when choosing fish for your reef aquarium is compatibility–compatibility not only with other fish but also with all of the other living things in the aquarium. It is imperative to buy only fish that are "invertebrate safe," because many fish common to the aquarium hobby will eat corals, shrimp, clams, or just about anything else in an aquarium that resembles meat. That's why fish that carry the "invertebrate-safe" label tend to be strictly algae eaters in the wild. Most of these same fish will learn to eat a variety of non-algal foods in an aquarium but still will not bother any of your other livestock.

There are other reasons why particular species might not be good for a reef tank even though they are not necessarily killers of cnidarians or other invertebrates. Some species get along well enough with invertebrates but will not get along well—will kill, if they get the chance—tankmates of their own or similar species. Addditionally, of course, some fish get too big for life in even fairly large tanks, so it is very important for you to get as much information as possible about a particular species you might be thinking of adding to your mini-reef.

When trying to decide how many fish to add, keep in mind that, as discussed earlier, it is your goal to keep nutrient levels as low as possible in the aquarium. Fish foods and fish wastes are very high in nutrients, so the addition of both to an aquarium should be kept at a minimum. That is why it is best to keep only a few fish even in large reef aquariums. It can be hard to keep yourself from adding more and more fish, but you'll be much better off in the long run—and often even in the short—if you keep the population small. It is ideal to have no more than one small to medium-size fish per 10 to 15 gallons of aquarium water. Obviously you can add more smaller-sized fish or fewer larger-sized fish, but the fewer the better.

When choosing fish you should always inquire about how long the fish has been in the store and whether it is eating. Fish are placed under a great deal of stress when they are shipped to wholesalers and stores and should be allowed to settle in for a few days. This way if any fish get sick or die from shipping stress or disease, it will happen at the store, not in your aquarium. Many store employees will not mind letting you watch a fish eat and will tell you what type of food the fish prefers.

Always remember that all fish are also subject to problems caused by parasites and diseases. However, most illnesses that your fish may get can be treated quite easily if they are recognized early enough. For this reason it is a good idea to pick up some literature on the subject and take the time to read it thoroughly. You should also always remember, if you do require some sort of medication in the future, that many fish medications, especially those that contain copper, are deadly to invertebrates. So if you have to use medications, make sure to use types that are labeled as being safe for invertebrates.

After purchasing a fish (or any other livestock) and transporting it to your aquarium, make sure to properly acclimate it to your aquarium's water before release. The best way to do this is to put the fish into a large bowl or a bucket with the water it was transported in. Next, take a piece of small-diameter tubing (airline tubing from the aquarium store works well) and start a siphon from the aquarium into the container. The slower the flow the better, so you may want to tie a loose knot in the tubing or otherwise constrict it to reduce the flow rate. Once three or four times the original volume of water has

This small black saddle anemonefish has taken up residence in a very large long-tentacle anemone.

Left: A lawnmower blenny, Salarias fasciatus—*not very prepossessing in looks but one of the best algae eaters there is, constantly darting around the aquarium stripping away microalgae from rocks and glass. Middle: A watchman goby,* Gobiosoma *sp.* Photo by Gary Lange *Right:* Zebrasoma flavescens, *the yellow tang, regarded by many as the best surgeonfish species for a mini-reef aquarium.* Photo by Mark Smith

been siphoned down and added to the container, the fish can be released into the aquarium. People who are not so patient usually just scoop a couple of cups of aquarium water into the bag with the fish, wait a few minutes, then repeat until the bag is full. You'll have more success being patient. It is very important to do this with all fish going into the aquarium in order for them to slowly adjust from the store's water to your aquarium's water, which will almost certainly be at least slightly different in salinity, temperature, and pH. Safer yet would be to subject new fish acquisitions to a quarantine period of at least a week or so before adding them to your aquarium.

There are literally hundreds of species of fish that are suitable for reef aquariums, and it would take an entire book to discuss all of them in detail. Instead, information is provided about a few of the groups of fish that are best for beginners. All of these groups of fish tend to have members that are relatively hardy and will not harm any of your invertebrate livestock.

Damselfish

Damselfish are some of the best small fish for the reef aquarium. They are exceptionally hardy and come in a wide variety of bright colors as well as black and white. They are also some of the least expensive marine fish available. The only problem you may have is aggressiveness. These fish will often become territorial in an aquarium and will chase and fend off other fish, especially other damselfish. For this reason it is best to never add more than a few of them to an aquarium, even though they are small in size.

Not always thought of as damselfish although they're in the same family are the clownfish, or anemonefish, because of their association with those animals. Clownfish are for the most part good-looking fish, so they make good additions even to tanks that don't house a sea anemone. Clowns usually don't bother other types of fish in the aquarium, but they'll readily battle other clownfish, even clownfish of different species. One big exception to this behavioral rule is with mated pairs; pairs will usually stick together for life, even in an aquarium.

Blennies and Gobies

Blennies and gobies make great additions because they are small and hardy, and many will eat algae off live rock and glass. They also are very interesting to watch, and each type has its own distinctive personality. While there are dozens of species, many of which look nothing like the others, almost without exception they are peaceful in most situations and won't bother

other fish or invertebrates. However, like many other types of fish, they may at times be aggressive toward members of their own species or similar blennies or gobies. Again, it is best to keep their numbers low and to learn what you can about each particular species.

Tangs

Tangs, or surgeonfish, are among the most popular fish in the hobby, and many are safe for your reef aquarium. They are relatively large and very colorful, and most are very intelligent and personable. Many tangs will also quickly get used to eating from your hand. The only problem with these fish is that they usually don't like others of their own species and sometimes don't like other types of tangs either. You can try to put three or more of the same species together (many school in the wild) but never put just two of the same species together. If you want more than one it is best to try tangs that have very different colors and body shapes (such as a yellow tang and a blue or regal tang).

Pygmy Angelfish

The last group of fish to mention here are the pygmy angelfish. These fish come in a wide variety of colors and are all very attractive. As the name implies, they also stay small in size, unlike their large cousins the "regular" angelfish (which are not invertebrate safe). However, like many of these other types of fish, they tend to fight with others of the same species, so don't try to put two conspecifics together in one aquarium.

Undesirables

There are many fish that you should avoid putting into your reef aquarium for a variety of reasons, so be careful. A few of these are the "regular" angelfish, which tend to be sponge eaters; the butterflyfish, which are commonly sponge and coral eaters; triggerfish, which can eat coral and other invertebrates; and parrotfish which also are coral eaters. Groupers and lionfish won't eat corals, but they will eat some other invertebrates such as shrimp, and when they get big enough they'll eat any small fish around. Many wrasses will also eat small invertebrates such as snails and shrimp and should be avoided. The point is, make sure you know what you're adding before you add!

Right: Pterois volitans, *one of the lionfish species; bizarre, but not a good candidate for the mini-reef tank containing small fish.* Photo by Mark Smith

Above: The dwarf angelfish Centropyge argi. Photo by Mark Smith

Below: Balistes vetula, *one of the coral-crunching triggerfish.* Photo by Mark Smith

Left: Chaetodon auriga, *the threadfin butterflyfish; like most other butterflyfish species, not welcome in a mini-reef aquarium.* Photo by Ed Taylor

Maintaining Your Reef Aquarium

N ow that you have started stocking your aquarium it's time to start doing everything necessary to maintain it properly. Your ultimate goal is to "get to know" your aquarium and to understand the needs of your livestock. As time passes this will happen if you spend time working on your aquarium and pay close attention to its inhabitants. You will slowly but surely learn the behavior and needs of each creature, as well as the whole aquarium as a miniaturized ecosystem. From the starting of your aquarium and into the future it is of the utmost importance to develop the proper maintenance habits and to be consistent in the aquarium's care in order to ensure years of enjoyment as a reef aquarium keeper.

FEEDING YOUR LIVESTOCK

A good place to start on the subject of maintenance is feeding your fish and other livestock. Most fish suitable for a reef aquarium will eat a wide variety of prepared foods, including flake food, brine shrimp, and bloodworms. Tangs and other more herbivorous species will also eat dried algae-based products. Still others may not eat anything you give them at all and will find their own food by sifting tiny animals from the substrate or by nibbling algae off the rocks and glass. The point is that you should find out what your particular fish need to keep them healthy. It is a good idea to try a wide variety of foods to see what they prefer. If they will eat more than one type, you should try to give them some of each periodically to vary their diet and ensure that they are receiving all of the different nutrients they need to thrive.

If you are in the process of cycling the aquarium you will most likely have added a couple of damselfish to start. It is easiest to start with a quality flake food, feeding them once a day. When you try to figure out how much to give, take a look at how small the fish are and then picture how small their little stomachs are. Not big at all. They are also cold- blooded, so they require much less fuel to keep going. No matter how hungry they may act, only give them a small pinch of food a day.

As the building of your reef progresses and you add more fish, the main thing to remember concerning feeding is to *never* overfeed any of your fish at any time. You should always give your fish only as much as they can eat in a couple of minutes no matter how many fish you end up with. Excess food that doesn't get eaten promptly tends to get caught by filters or settles on the bottom and between rocks to rot. This can in turn lead to the production of excess ammonia and other unwanted substances and nutrients, especially phosphates, which are present in all foods. As discussed earlier, ammonia is poisonous to all of your livestock, and elevated phosphate levels in your reef aquarium will cause unwanted algae to grow and can cause serious health problems for stony corals.

As far as other livestock goes, most crabs and shrimps that you may add to your aquarium will have no trouble finding their own food and will not require additional food sources. Other types of livestock such as corals and anemones will derive most or all of the nutrients they need directly from the aquarium's water and from the lighting system (as long as you have the proper lights). However, exceptions to this are made on occasion. Some corals and anemones can be fed small bits of prepared foods by hand, or by using an eyedropper or syringe, and others will actually eat small feeder fish such as tuffy minnows (also called bluntnose minnows) or goldfish. Just keep in mind that 99% of the time they don't really require it. In fact, if you don't have excellent water quality and a very efficient protein skimmer I would suggest that you don't feed any invertebrates at all, since any food added will directly or indirectly raise the overall nutrient level in the aquarium. The key here is to learn as much about your invertebrates as possible and to keep from feeding them if they don't require it or at least to never overfeed any of them.

TESTING THE WATER QUALITY

Test kits made for checking various aspects of water quality can be somewhat expensive and troublesome to use, but buying and using them is much better in the long run than dealing with sick or dead livestock. Even after the aquarium has cycled it is a good idea to test your water frequently for at least the next couple of months. Most importantly, test for ammonia and nitrite. The results of these tests should give you a good indication of how well your biological filter is working. Knowing this is essential, because both ammonia and nitrite are deadly even at low concentrations and can rise quickly as you start to add more fish to the aquarium. Once you feel confident that everything is going well you may start testing less frequently. It is also beneficial to regularly test as many other parameters as possible. These include pH, alkalinity, calcium levels, nitrate, and anything else that can be measured with the available home test kits. Look at the chart below for information on acceptable levels of common things that you can test for with home test kits. If for some reason you decide to use tap water in your aquarium in the future (which, again, is a bad idea) it is also a good idea to test it for any problems *before* adding it to the aquarium. Even "good" tap water commonly has ammonia, phosphates, and copper in it, all of which are bad for your livestock.

Following is a general guide to the values for which you'll most often be testing.
Specific gravity: 1.022 to 1.030, optimally 1.022
Temperature: 70 to 85F, optimally 75F
Ammonia: zero
Nitrite: zero
Nitrate: less than 40ppm, optimally as low as possible
pH: 8.0 to 8.4
Alkalinity: 2.5 to 3.5 meq/l or 7 to 10dKH, optimally 3.5 meq/l or 10 dKH
Calcium: 375 to 475 mg/l, optimally 475 mg/l
Phosphate: near zero, optimally zero

CLEANING THE AQUARIUM AND FILTERS

The parts of the aquarium that most obviously require maintenance are the viewing surfaces, of course. Every reef aquarium acts differently, but in all of them the upright transparent surfaces will eventually get covered by various types of microalgae and later by coralline algae if you do not take action against it. There are several ways to clean those surfaces, with the method used usually determined by the stubbornness of the algae and whether the surfaces are glass or acrylic. Acrylic scratches more easily than glass, so the materials used on it to remove algal growths must be less abrasive or sharp than those used on glass. There are a number of different algae-removing devices on the market; you should have at least one type on hand. When using any cutting/slicing instrument like a sharp blade of any type, you have to be very careful about the aquarium's seals. Don't ever run a razor scraper up the corner of the aquarium or cut the silicone seals that hold the glass together in any way. The hazards involved with damaging the seals are obvious.

Fingerprints and dust need to be removed from the outside of the aquarium periodically. I've found that the best tool for this job is a small squeegee. You can use plain water if you wish, or a real glass cleaner for tough spots. If you use a commercial cleaner, you *must* make sure that none of the cleaner gets into the aquarium, as most cleaners have a large amount of ammonia and a bunch of other nasty stuff in them.

The substrate in the aquarium should also be cleaned on a regular basis, at least monthly. Often the substrate in the aquarium will look relatively clean at the surface, but what you must remember is that a considerable amount of detritus settles into it and collects in it over time. While many aquarists proceed on the basis that if it's out of sight it's no problem, it actually is a problem. Detritus, especially in the form of fish wastes and excess fish foods, is very high in nutrients. If wastes are allowed to accumulate in the substrate they will leach harmful nutrients into the water. To clean the substrate you'll need a siphon designed for that job. These are wide clear plastic tubes that have a narrower hose attached to one end. When the large end is shoved into the substrate the siphon will suck most, if not all, of the detritus out. Since the siphon is big at the intake end and small at the discharge end, it is strong enough to suck up detritus but not strong enough to suck up the substrate. The substrate just swirls around in the cylinder and is then left in place, freed of its lighter particles.

Because you won't want to move all of your live rock to clean up any detritus that has settled behind it, you'll need a strong powerhead to blow it out. Just use a powerhead like a small-scale leaf blower to blast detritus out from under and behind the rocks so that it can be trapped by your mechanical filter(s). If there is a large amount in the back then it will be best to do this before you siphon the substrate. If you first turn off all of the other pumps and filters that circulate water in the aquarium, much of the detritus will settle on the substrate in the front of the aquarium, where you can get to it with the siphon.

The next step is cleaning or replacing filter media in mechanical filters. In mechanical filters that use a sponge you should remove the sponge and rinse it thoroughly as often as you can make yourself do it; even once a day isn't overdoing it in large aquariums. This helps to remove detritus as fast as it is collected by the filters, which in turn helps keep nutrient levels at a minimum. Fish feces and leftover foods simply don't have time to break down and dissolve into the water. You should perform this task at an absolute minimum of once a week. For mechanical filters that use replaceable media you should keep in mind that the media need to be replaced *before* they look filthy. If you wait until they look really dirty, most of the material that they initially trapped has probably dissolved back into the aquarium already, which of course leads to higher nutrient levels. For certain canister-type filters it is possible to reuse the cartridges instead of replacing them regularly. The cartridges can be removed from the filter and soaked in water and bleach overnight. This treatment dissolves away virtually all traces of anything that was on the cartridge. The cartridge can then be rinsed thoroughly, dried, and later reused. Just make sure that you absolutely, positively, do not get even the tiniest amount of bleach back into the aquarium, as it is very poisonous. If after rinsing and drying the cartridges they still have even the trace of any odor of bleach, you need to place them in some water and add a bit of your chlorine/chloramine remover to neutralize any remnant bleach. The best plan is to go ahead and buy a couple of extra cartridges and rotate them out with dirty ones while they are being cleaned. That way there is no downtime for the filter itself.

Taking care of the protein skimmer requires a little more attention. If adjusted properly your skimmer should produce a thick and relatively dry-looking dark foam. If it begins to make a wet, clear foam either the water flow rate is too high or the air flow rate is too low. If it makes no foam for a period of days, it may also need to be adjusted. Basically every skimmer acts differently on every aquarium, and all will almost certainly require you to monitor and adjust them through trial and error.

Always make sure that all of the "working" parts of the skimmer stay in good shape. For venturi-type skimmers this means that the pump that drives it should be running properly and that the air intake for the venturi valve should be cleaned out periodically to ensure that the airflow isn't impeded. For countercurrent-type skimmers the driving pump should also be working properly and the air pump should be working properly as well. Because these skimmers produce the greatest amount of foam when the bubbles in the skimmer are smallest, the airstones should be replaced every few weeks (or as often as needed to maintain the production of tiny bubbles). Wooden airstones seem to do the best job, but they deteriorate relatively quickly in the salty water. For both types you should obviously empty the collection cup as it gets full of the liquid formed from the foam. You should also wash off any collected solid material in the cup and on its cap.

Keep in mind that the skimmer will normally not produce any foam at all for the first several weeks, because there is nothing to strip out of the water. Even after the aquarium and the skimmer have been running for months, many times the skimmer will periodically cease to produce foam for no apparent reason and then will later start to produce it again. This doesn't necessarily mean that anything is wrong with the aquarium or the skimmer—it's just a symptom of the constant changes that occur in the aquarium over time.

USING ADDITIVES

A task required in the maintenance of reef aquariums is the periodic use of additives, most importantly calcium, strontium, and iodine. The addition of calcium optimally should depend upon test results, because testing the actual concentration of calcium in the water is the only way to really know how much or how often to add it. However, most of the time hobbyists simply follow the directions provided by the manufacturer of the calcium additive itself. All of them provide some guideline as to when and how much to add based on an "average" aquarium, but you can use a little common sense to adjust to your own aquarium. If you don't have many stony corals, clams, or other animals that use calcium in their structures, you should cut back on the dosage. Conversely, if you have a tank full of calcium-using animals you may need to add even more than the manufacturer says. The same logic follows with the addition of both strontium and iodine. The more animals you have that use these elements, the more you'll need to add.

OTHER DUTIES

On nearly a daily basis you will need to observe the water level in your aquarium. High-output light systems, especially those with cooling fans, can cause high rates of evaporation. The water level will therefore constantly drop in the aquarium and the salinity will constantly rise, because only pure water evaporates and the salt is left behind. For this reason it is important to add replacement water to the aquarium frequently. This replacement water should be a high-quality fresh, not salt, water.

On a monthly basis you should perform a partial water change. This can be done simply by throwing out the water siphoned out of the aquarium when cleaning the substrate, then replacing it with newly made salt water. During the cleaning you will probably siphon out anywhere from 10 to 20 percent of the aquarium's volume, which is actually the recommended volume of a monthly water change. After you have removed the "old" water, mix up a new batch of salt water following the same steps that were discussed earlier and add it to the aquarium. The only difference is that once you have livestock in your aquarium you'll have to make up new salt water in a bucket instead of in the aquarium itself.

Now you have cleaned the substrate and done the recommended water change all in one step. These water changes help to dilute the aquarium's "old" water, thus reducing the concentration of any pollutants that may have entered the aquarium. These water changes also replenish beneficial trace element concentrations as well as those of other substances.

Many hobbyists have started the practice of using carbon only periodically instead of constantly and are having good results. In these cases a large amount (about 1 cup to every 25 gallons of water) of fresh carbon is used only once every few weeks, and only for a period of a few days. It is most convenient and easiest to remember if you'll use the carbon just before a water change. This practice was developed by reef aquarium hobbyists because carbon sucks not only many harmful substances out of the water but also many trace elements and other beneficial compounds. So if you'll use it a few days before a water change and remove it immediately preceding the change, when you do the water change and replenish the aquarium's trace element concentrations the carbon won't be there to remove them.

On a longer term basis, it is also important to clean and lubricate any pumps that require it. Large pumps are quite expensive, but when cared for properly they will last for years and years. Always follow the manufacturer's directions on how and when to perform maintenance on them.

You will also need to replace your fluorescent tubes at regular intervals. While they may appear to last for several years, all high-output lamps change in color over time. The longer they burn the more their spectrum shifts away from their original color and the less effective they become for keeping photosynthetic livestock. Depending on the type(s) of lamp used, it has been suggested that VHO and metal halide lamps be replaced after no longer than one year. Power compacts reportedly last a bit longer and may be usable for as long as a year and a half. Unfortunately, these changes are not really noticeable to the eye, and there is no real way to test whether your bulbs need replacing or not (unless you can find a spectrometer). Hobbyists who pay close attention to their livestock may notice changes in their behavior and appearance that signal the need for changes, but for the most part you'll just have to go by the manufacturer's suggestions. When changing lamps you should also remember to give any cooling fans a good cleaning. After a year's time the fan's blades and motor will usually be covered by dust and will need to be cleaned with a toothbrush or other similar tool.

In closing, by now you should realize that while all this may seem a bit overwhelming there are really only a few basic things to remember. Keep your aquarium clean. Do everything you can to keep nutrient levels as low as possible. Keep the concentrations of bad things at a minimum and the concentrations of good things at acceptable levels. Take good care of your equipment. And last, but not least, give your photosynthetic livestock plenty of proper lighting.